Service Transition based on ITIL V3® -

C000067168

Other publications by Van Haren Publishing

Van Haren Publishing (VHP) specializes in titles on Best Practices, methods and standards within IT management, Architecture (Enterprise and IT), business management and project management.

These publications are grouped in series, eg: *ITSM Library* (on behalf of ITSMF International), *Best Practice* and *IT Management Topics*. VHP is also publisher on behalf of leading companies and institutions, eg The Open Group, IPMA-NL, CA, Getronics, Pink Elephant. At the time of going to press the following books are available:

IT (Service) Management / IT Governance

ITSM, ITIL® V3 and ITIL® V2

Foundations of IT Service Management – based on ITIL® V3 (English, Dutch, German; French, Japanese and Spanish editions)

Introduction to IT Service Management (ITIL V3, English)

IT Service Management based on ITIL V3 – A Pocket Guide (English, Dutch, German, Italian; French, Japanese and Spanish editions)

Foundations of IT Service Management based on ITIL® (ITIL V2), (English, Dutch, French, German, Spanish, Japanese, Chinese, Danish, Italian, Korean, Russian, Arabic; also available as a CD-ROM)

Implementing Service and Support Management Processes (English)

Release and Control for IT Service Management, based on ITIL® – A Practitioner Guide (English)

ISO/IEC 20000

ISO/IEC 20000 – An Introduction (English, German)

Implementing ISO/IEC 20000 Certification (English)

ISO/IEC 20000 – A Pocket Guide (English, Italian, German, Spanish, Portuguese)

ISO 27001 and ISO 17799

Information Security based on ISO 27001 and ISO 17799 – A Management Guide (English)

Implementing Information Security based on ISO 27001 and ISO 17799 – A Management Guide (English)

COBIT

IT Governance based on COBIT4.1® – A Management Guide (English, German, Japanese)

IT Service CMM

IT Service CMM – A Pocket Guide (English)

ASL and BiSL

ASL – A Framework for Application Management (English, German)

ASL – Application Services Library – A Management Guide (English, Dutch)

BiSL – A Framework for Business Information Management (Dutch, English)

BiSL – Business information Services Library – A Management Guide (Dutch; English)

ISPL

IT Services Procurement op basis van ISPL (Dutch)

IT Services Procurement based on ISPL – A Pocket Guide (English)

Other IT Management titles:

De RfP voor IT-outsourcing (Dutch; English version due Spring 2008)

Decision- en Controlfactoren voor IT-Sourcing (Dutch)

Defining IT Success through the Service Catalogue (English)

Frameworks for IT Management – An introduction (English, Japanese; German)

Frameworks for IT Management – A Pocket Guide (English, German, Dutch)

Implementing IT Governance (English)

Implementing leading standards for IT management (English, Dutch)

IT Service Management global best practices, volume 1 (English)

IT Service Management Best Practices, volume 1, 2, 3 and 4 (Dutch)

ITSM from hell! / ITSM from hell based on Not ITIL (English)

ITSMP – The IT Strategy Management Process (English)

Metrics for IT Service Management (English, Russian)

Service Management Process Maps (English)

Six Sigma for IT Management (English)

Six Sigma for IT Management – A Pocket Guide (English)

MOF/MSF

MOF – Microsoft Operations Framework, A Pocket Guide (Dutch, English, French, German, Japanese)

MSF – Microsoft Solutions Framework, A Pocket Guide (English, German)

Architecture (Enterprise and IT)

TOGAF, The Open Group Architecture Framework – A Management Guide (English)

The Open Group Architecture Framework – 2007 Edition (English, official publication of TOG)

TOGAF™ Version 8 Enterprise Edition – Study Guide (English, official publication of TOG)

TOGAF™ Version 8.1.1 Enterprise Edition –A Pocket Guide (English, official publication of TOG)

Business Management

ISO 9000

ISO 9001:2000 – The Quality Management Process (English)

EFQM

The EFQM excellence model for Assessing Organizational Performance – A Management Guide (English)

SqEME®

Process management based on SqEME® (English)

SqEME® – A Pocket Guide (English, Dutch)

Project/Programme/Risk Management

ICB/NCB

NCB Versie 3– Nederlandse Competence Baseline (Dutch, on behalf of IPMA-NL)

Projectmanagement op basis van NCB V3 – IPMA-C en IPMA-D (Dutch)

PRINCE2™

Project Management based on PRINCE2™– Edition 2005 (English, Dutch, German)

PRINCE2™ – A No Nonsense Management Guide (English)

PRINCE2™ voor opdrachtgevers – Management Guide (Dutch)

MINCE®

MINCE® – A Framework for Organizational Maturity (English)

MSP

Programme Management based on MSP (English, Dutch)

Programme Management based on MSP – A Management Guide (English)

M_o_R

Risk Management based on M_o_R – A Management Guide (English)

Other publications on project management:

Wegwijzer voor methoden bij Projectvolwassenheid (Dutch: fall 2008)

Het Project Management Office – Management Guide (Dutch)

For the latest information on VHP publications, visit our website: www.vanharen.net

Service Transition
based on ITIL® V3

A Management Guide

Van Haren
PUBLISHING

Colophon

Title:	Service Transition based on ITIL V3® - A Management Guide
Authors:	Jan van Bon (Chief Editor, Inform-IT)
	Arjen de Jong (co-author, Inform-IT)
	Axel Kolthof (co-author, Inform-IT)
	Mike Pieper (co-author, Inform-IT)
	Ruby Tjassing (co-author, Inform-IT)
	Annelies van der Veen (co-author, Inform-IT)
	Tieneke Verheijen (co-author, Inform-IT)
Copy editor:	Jayne Wilkinson
Publisher:	Van Haren Publishing, Zaltbommel, www.vanharen.net
Design & layout:	CO2 Premedia bv, Amersfoort - NL
ISBN:	9789087531263
Edition:	First edition, first impression, June 2008

Foreword

ITIL receives more and more attention on a global scale, with many companies adopting its principles. In that respect, ITIL version 2 has done a good job. The update of ITIL in version 3, released in June 2007, has caused some concern for many of these companies, since it built on the idea that companies had already achieved results with version 2 content. In practice however, most companies are still working their way through the basic principles of ITIL. For that reason, the "Foundations of IT Service Management – based on ITIL V3" was developed, offering a comprehensive but easy-to-understand source of information on ITIL. This title is now widely used as the authoritative guide on ITIL V3 in training situations and in implementations.

Apart from offering the market a summarized, easy-to-understand source on ITIL V3, that can be used for a step-by-step approach, many companies focus on a subset of the ITIL best practices. That is why we developed a series of ITIL Management Guides, focusing on the processes, procedures, and functions, from each of the phases of the ITIL V3 Lifecycle. This enables companies to focus on those phases that are of primary concern to them.

Each of the five ITIL V3 Management Guides is structured the same way as the successful Foundations book: it separates the Lifecycle information from the single process, procedure and function components, enabling organizations to take their own approach and still adopt ITIL best practices.

The content of each guide was derived from the Foundations book, which ensures that you'll find the same high quality as usual. This means that all content has been peer-reviewed in a rigorous way, making sure that it completely aligns to ITIL V3, but also that it was the best, concise and comprehensive summary of ITIL V3 core content that could be achieved.

I'm convinced that this new management guide will provide an excellent reference tool for practitioners, students and others who want to have a practical guide on the key ITIL V3 concepts.

Jan van Bon
Chief Editor

Acknowledgements

This Management Guide is a compilation of the itSMF publication "Foundations of IT Service Management - Based on ITIL V3". Thus, the international review team that reviewed "Foundations of IT Service Management", has contributed indirectly to this Management Guide. We would like to thank all reviewers once again for their detailed review which improved the quality of both books significantly.

The review team consists of:
- John van Beem, ISES International, Netherlands
- Aad Brinkman, Apreton, Netherlands
- Peter Brooks, PHMB Consulting, itSMF South Africa
- Rob van der Burg, Microsoft, Netherlands
- Judith Cremers, Getronics PinkRoccade Educational Services, Netherlands
- Robert Falkowitz, Concentric Circle Consulting, itSMF Switzerland
- Rosario Fondacaro, Quint Wellington Redwood, Italy
- Peter van Gijn, LogicaCMG, Netherlands
- Jan Heunks, ICT Partners, Netherlands
- Linh Ho, Compuware Corporation, USA
- Ton van der Hoogen, ToTZ Diensten, Netherlands
- Kevin Holland, NHS, UK
- Matiss Horodishtiano, Amdocs, itSMF Israel
- Wim Hoving, BHVB, Netherlands
- Brian Johnson, CA, USA
- Georges Kemmerling, Quint Wellington Redwood, Netherlands
- Kirstie Magowan, itSMF New Zealand
- Steve Mann, OpSys - SM2, itSMF Belgium
- Reiko Morita, Ability InterBusiness Solutions, Inc., Japan
- Jürgen Müller, Marval Benelux, Netherlands
- Ingrid Ouwerkerk, Getronics PinkRoccade Educational Services, Netherlands
- Ton Sleutjes, CapGemini, Netherlands
- Maxime Sottini, Innovative Consulting, itSMF Italy
- Takashi Yagi, Hitachi Ltd., itSMF Japan

Given the desire for a broad consensus in the IT Service Management field, new developments, additional material and contributions from ITSM professionals who have worked with ITIL version 3 are welcome. They will be discussed by the editors and where appropriate incorporated into new editions. Comments can be sent to the Chief Editor, Jan van Bon, email: j.van.bon@inform-it.org.

Contents

Introduction

1.1 Background

Developments in IT have had a tremendous effect on the business market during the last decade. Since the appearance of extremely powerful hardware, highly versatile software and super-fast networks, all connected to each other worldwide, organizations have been able to develop their information-dependent products and services to a greater extent, and to bring them to the market much faster. These developments have marked the transition of the industrial age into the **information age**. In the information age, everything has become faster and more dynamic, and everything is connected.

Traditional hierarchical organizations often have difficulties in responding to this rapidly changing market, and this has led to current trends for organizations to become flatter and more flexible. The focus has shifted from vertical silos to horizontal **processes**, and decision-making powers are increasingly bestowed on the employees. It is against this background that the work processes of IT service management have arisen.

An important advantage of process-oriented organizations is that processes can be designed to support a **customer-oriented approach**. This has made the alignment between the IT organization (responsible for supplying information) and the customer (responsible for using these information systems in their business) increasingly significant. Over the last couple of years, this trend has attracted attention under the title of **Business-IT Alignment (BITA)**.

As organizations gained more experience with the **process-oriented approach** of IT service management, it became clear that the process must be managed coherently.

Furthermore, it was obvious that the introduction of a process-oriented work method meant a big change for the primarily line and project-oriented organizations. Culture and change management proved to be crucial elements for a successful organizational design.

Another important lesson learned was that the IT organization must not lose itself in a process culture. Just like the one-sided project-oriented organization, a one-sided process-oriented organization was not the optimum type of business. Balance was, as always, the magic word. In addition, it became clear that the customer-oriented approach required that an **end-to-end** and **user-centric** approach must be followed: it was of no help to the user to know that "the server was still in operation" if the information system was not available at the user's workplace. IT services must be viewed in a larger context. The need for the recognition of the **Service Lifecycle**, and the management of IT services in light of that lifecycle, became a concern.

Due to the fast growing dependency of business upon information, the quality of information services in companies is being increasingly subjected to stricter **internal and external requirements**. The role of **standards** is getting more and more important, and **frameworks** of "best practices" help with the development of a management system to meet these requirements. Organizations that are not in control of their processes, will not be able to realize great results on the level of the Service Lifecycle and the end-to-end-management of those services. Organizations that do not have their internal organization in order, will also not achieve great results. For these reasons, all these aspects are handled alongside each other in the course of this book.

1.2 Why this book

This book offers detailed information for those who are responsible for strategic information issues, as well as for the (much larger) group who are responsible for setting up and executing the delivery of the information systems. This is supported by both the description of the Service Lifecycle, as documented in ITIL version 3, and by the description of the processes that are associated with it. The ITIL core books are very extensive, and can be used for a thorough study of contemporary best practices. This management guide provides the reader with an easy-to-read comprehensive introduction to the broad library of ITIL core books, to support the understanding and the further distribution of ITIL as an industry standard. Once this understanding of the structure of ITIL has been gained, the reader can use the core books for a more detailed understanding and guidance for their daily practice.

1.3 Organizations

Several organizations are involved in the maintenance of ITIL as a description of the "best practice" in the IT service management field.

OGC

Initially ITIL was a product of the CCTA, a UK Government Organization. On 1 April 2001 the CCTA was incorporated into the OGC, which thus became the new owner of ITIL. The aim of the OGC is to help its clients (within the UK Government) with the modernization of their procurement activities and the improvement of their services, by, among other things, making the best possible use of IT: "OGC aims to modernize procurement in government, and deliver substantial value for money improvements". The OGC promotes the use of 'best practices' in numerous areas, such as project management, program management, procurement, risk management and IT service management. For this reason the OGC itself has published several series of books (Libraries) which have been written by (international) experts from different companies and organizations.

itSMF

The target group for this publication is anyone who is involved or interested in IT service management. A professional organization, working on the development of the IT service management field, has been created especially for this target group.
In 1991 the Information Technology Service Management Forum (itSMF), originally known as the Information Technology Infrastructure Management Forum (ITIMF), was set up as a UK association. In 1994, a sister-association was established in the Netherlands, following the UK example.

Since then, independent itSMF organizations have been set up in more than forty countries, spread across the globe, and the number of "chapters" continues to grow. All itSMF organizations operate under the umbrella organization, itSMF International (itSMF-I).

itSMF is aimed at the entire professional area of IT service management. It promotes the exchange of information and experiences that IT organizations can use to improve their service provision. itSMF is also involved in the use and quality of the various standards and methods that are important in the field. One of these standards is ITIL. itSMF International has an agreement with OGC and APM Group on the promotion of the use of ITIL. itSMF International has an agreement with OGC and APM Group on the promotion of the use of ITIL.

APM Group

In 2006, OGC contracted the management of ITIL rights, the certification of ITIL exams and accreditation of training organizations to the APM Group (APMG), a commercial organization. APMG defines the certification and accreditation for the ITIL exams, and published the new certification system (see Section 2.1: ITIL exams).

Exam bodies

The Dutch foundation Examen Instituut voor Informatica (EXIN) and the English Information Systems Examination Board (ISEB, part of the BCS: the British Computer Society) cooperated in the development and provision of certification for IT service management. For many years they were the only bodies that provided ITIL exams. With the contracting of APMG by OGC, the responsibility for ITIL exams is now with APMG. To support the world-wide delivery of these ITIL exams, APMG has accredited a number of exam bodies: EXIN, BCS/ISEB, and Loyalist College, Canada.

1.4   Structure of the book

Chapter 2, introduces the Service Lifecycle, in the context of IT service management and IT governance. It discusses principles of organizational maturity, and the benefits and risks of following a service management framework. This chapter ends with the introduction of the Service Lifecycle.

In Chapters 3 the Service Transition lifecycle phase is discussed in detail, in a standardized structure.

Chapter 4 provides general information on principles of processes, teams, roles, functions, positions, tools, and other elements of interest.

In chapter 5, the processes and functions of Service Transition are described in detail. Each of these processes and functions is described in terms of:
- Introduction
- Activities, methods and techniques
- Interfaces, inputs and outputs
- Metrics and Key Performance Indicators (KPIs)
- Implementation, with Critical Success Factors (CSFs), challenges, risks and traps

The appendices provide useful sources for the reader. A reference list of used sources is provided, as well as the official ITIL Glossary and a list with acronyms. The book ends with an extensive index of relevant terms that will support the reader in finding relevant text elements.

CHAPTER 2

Introduction to the Service Lifecycle

2.1   Introduction to ITIL

In the 1980s the quality of service provided by both internal and external IT companies to UK government departments was of such a level that the CCTA (Central Computer and Telecommunications Agency, now the Office of Government Commerce, OGC) was instructed by the Government to develop a standard approach for an efficient and effective delivery of IT services. This was to be an approach which was independent of the suppliers (whether internal or external). The result of this instruction was the development and publication of the **Information Technology Infrastructure Library™** (ITIL). ITIL is made up of a collection of "best practices" found across the range of IT service providers.

ITIL offers a systematic approach to the delivery of quality of IT services. It gives a detailed description of most of the important processes in an IT organization, and includes checklists for tasks, procedures and responsibilities which can be used as a basis for tailoring to the needs of individual organizations.

At the same time, the broad coverage of ITIL also provides a helpful reference guide for many areas, which can be used to develop new improvement goals for an IT organization, enabling it to grow and mature.

Over the years, ITIL has become much more than a series of useful books about IT service management. The framework for the "best practice" in IT service management is promoted and further developed by advisors, trainers and suppliers of technologies or products. Since the nineties, ITIL represents not only the theoretical framework, but the approach and philosophy shared by the people who work with it in practice.

Being an extended framework of best practices for IT service management itself, the advantages and disadvantages of frameworks in general, described in Section 2.5, are also applicable to ITIL. Of course, ITIL was developed because of the advantages mentioned earlier. Many of the pointers from "best practices" are intended to avoid potential problems, or, should they occur after all, to solve them.

ITIL exams

In 2007 the APM Group launched a new certification scheme for ITIL, based on ITIL version 3. ITIL version 2 will be maintained for a transition period, continuing until the year 2008. **ITIL version 2** has qualifications on three levels:
* **Foundation Certificate** in IT Service Management
* **Practitioner Certificate** in IT Service Management
* **Manager Certificate** in IT Service Management

Until 2000, some 60,000 ITIL certificates had been distributed and by 2006 the number had reached 500,000 certificates .

For **ITIL version 3** a new system of qualifications has been set up. There are four qualification levels:
* Foundation Level
* Intermediate Level (Lifecycle Stream & Capability Stream)
* ITIL Diploma
* Advanced Service Management Professional Diploma

For more information about the ITIL V3 Qualification Scheme, see http://www.itil-officialsite.com/Qualifications/ITILV3QualificationScheme.asp.

2.2 IT governance

With the growing role of information, information systems and IT service management, the management requirements for IT grew as well. These requirements focus on two aspects: the compliance with internal and external policies, laws and regulations, and the provision of added value to the stakeholders of the organization. IT governance is still a very young discipline, with no more than a few acknowledged standards or frameworks available. In contrast, there are many different definitions of IT governance available. A definition that receives a lot of support is the one by Van Grembergen:

> *IT governance* consists of a comprehensive framework of structures, processes and relational mechanisms. Structures involve the existence of responsible functions such as IT executives and accounts, and a diversity of IT Committees. Processes refer to strategic IT decision-making and monitoring. Relational mechanisms include business/IT participation and partnerships, strategic dialogue and shared learning.

There is a clear distinction between governance and management, suggesting that governance enables the creation of a setting in which others can manage their tasks effectively (Sohal & Fitzpatrick). So IT governance and IT management are two separate entities. IT service management can be considered to be part of the IT management domain, which leaves IT governance in the business or information management domain.

Although many frameworks are characterized as "IT Governance frameworks", such as COBIT and even ITIL, most of them are in fact management frameworks. There is at least one standard for IT Governance available: the local Australian standard for Corporate governance of information and communication technology (AS8015-2005).

2.3　Organizational maturity

From the moment **Richard Nolan** introduced his "staged model" for the application of IT in organizations in 1973, many people have used stepwise improvement models. These models were quickly recognized as suitable instruments for quality improvement programs, thereby helping organizations to climb up the maturity ladder.

Dozens of variations on the theme can easily be found, ranging from trades such as software development, acquisition, systems engineering, software testing, website development, data warehousing and security engineering, to help desks and knowledge management. Obviously the *kaizen* principle (improvement works best in smaller steps) was one that appealed to many.

After Nolan's staged model in 1973, the most appealing application of this modeling was found when the Software Engineering Institute (SEI) of Carnegie Mellon University, USA, published its Software Capability Maturity Model (SW-CMM). The CMM was copied and applied in most of the cases mentioned above, making CMM something of a standard in maturity modeling. The CMM was later followed by newer editions, including CMMI (CMM Integration).

Later, these models were applied in quality management models, like the European Foundation for Quality Management (EFQM). Apart from the broad quality management models, there are several other industry accepted practices, such as Six Sigma and Total Quality Management (TQM) which are complementary to ITIL.

The available standards, and frameworks of best practice, offer guidance for organizations in achieving "operational excellence" in IT service management. Depending upon their stage of development, organizations tend to require different kinds of guidance.

Maturity model: CMMI

In the IT industry, the process maturity improvement process is best known in the context of the **Capability Maturity Model Integration (CMMI)**. This process improvement method was developed by the Software Engineering Institute (SEI) of Carnegie Mellon University. CMMI provides both a staged and a continuous model. In the continuous representation, improvement is measured using capability levels. Maturity is measured for a particular process across an organization. In the staged representation, improvement is measured using maturity levels, for a set of processes across an organization.

The capability levels in the **CMMI continuous representation** are:

- **incomplete process** - a process that either is not performed or partially performed
- **performed process** - satisfies the specific goals of the process area
- **managed process** - a performed (capability level 1) process that has the basic infrastructure in place to support the process
- **defined process** - a managed (capability level 2) process that is tailored from the organization's set of standard processes according to the organization's tailoring guidelines, and contributes work products, measures and other process improvement information to the organizational process assets
- **quantitatively Managed process** - a defined (capability level 3) process that is controlled using statistical and other quantitative techniques
- **optimizing process** - a quantitatively managed (capability level 4) process that is improved based on an understanding of the common causes of variation inherent in the process

The **CMMI staged representation** model defines five maturity levels, each a layer in the base for the next phase in the ongoing process improvement, designated by the numbers 1 through 5:

1. **initial** - processes are ad hoc and chaotic
2. **managed** - the projects of the organization have ensured that processes are planned and executed in accordance with policy
3. **defined** - processes are well characterized and understood, and are described in standards, procedures, tools and methods

4. **quantitatively managed** - the organization and projects establish quantitative objectives for quality and process performance, and use them as criteria in managing processes

5. **optimizing** - focuses on continually improving process performance through incremental and innovative process and technological improvements

Many other maturity models were based on these structures, such as the Gartner Maturity Models. Most of these models are focused at capability maturity. Some others, like KPMG's World Class IT Maturity Model, take a different approach.

Standard: ISO/IEC 20000

Developing and maintaining a quality system which complies with the requirements of the ISO 9000 (ISO-9000:2000) series can be considered a tool for the organization to reach and maintain the system-focused (or "managed" in IT Service CMM) level of maturity. These ISO standards emphasize the definition, description and design of processes. For IT service management organizations, a specific ISO standard was produced: the ISO/ IEC 20000 (see Figure 2.1).

Figure 2.1 Overview of the ISO/IEC 20000 service management system

Customer maturity

When assessing the maturity of an organization, we cannot restrict ourselves to the service provider. The **level of maturity of the customer** (Figure 2.2) is also important. If there are large differences in maturity between the provider and the customer, then these will have to be considered to prevent a mismatch in the approach, methods and mutual expectations. Specifically, this affects the communication between the customer and the provider.

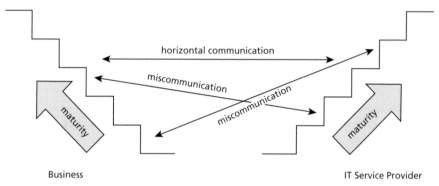

Figure 2.2 Communication and maturity levels: customer and provider

2.4   Benefits and risks of ITSM frameworks

The list below identifies some benefits and possible problems of using IT service management best practices. This list is not intended to be definitive, but is provided here as a basis for considering some of the benefits that can be achieved and some of the mistakes that can be made when using common process-based IT service management frameworks:

Benefits to the customer/user:
- The provision of IT services becomes more customer-focused and agreements about service quality improve the relationship.
- The services are described better, in customer language, and in more appropriate detail.
- Better management of the quality, availability, reliability and cost of the services are managed better.
- Communication with the IT organization is improved by agreeing on the points of contact.

Benefits to the IT organization:

- The IT organization develops a clearer structure, becomes more efficient, and is more focused on the corporate objectives.
- The IT organization is more in control of the infrastructure and services it has responsibility for, and changes become easier to manage.
- An effective process structure provides a framework for the effective outsourcing of elements of the IT services.
- Following best practices encourages a cultural change towards providing service, and supports the introduction of quality management systems based on the ISO 9000 series or on ISO/IEC 20000.
- Frameworks can provide coherent frames of reference for internal communication and communication with suppliers, and for the standardization and identification of procedures.

Potential problems/mistakes:

- The introduction can take a long time and require significant effort, and may require a change of culture in the organization; an overambitious introduction can lead to frustration because the objectives are never met.
- If process structures become an objective in themselves, the service quality may be adversely affected; in this scenario, unnecessary or over-engineered procedures are seen as bureaucratic obstacles, which are to be avoided where possible.
- There is no improvement in IT services due a fundamental lack of understanding about what the relevant processes should provide, what the appropriate performance indicators are, and how processes can be controlled.
- Improvement in the provision of services and cost reductions are insufficiently visible, because no baseline data was available for comparison and/or the wrong targets were identified.
- A successful implementation requires the involvement and commitment of personnel at all levels in the organization; leaving the development of the process structures to a specialist department may isolate that department in the organization and it may set a direction that is not accepted by other departments.
- If there is insufficient investment in appropriate training and support tools, justice will not be done to the processes and the service will not be improved; additional resources and personnel may be needed in the short term if the organization is already overloaded by routine IT service management activities which may not be using "best practices".

2.5   Service Lifecycle: concept and overview

The information provision role and system has grown and changed since the launch of ITIL version 2 (in 2000/02). IT supports and is part of an increasing number of goods and services. In the business world, the information provision role has changed as well: IT's role is no longer just supporting, but has become the baseline for the creation of business value.

ITIL version 3 intends to include and provide insight into IT's new role in all its complexity and dynamics. To that end, a new service management approach has been chosen that does not center around processes, but focuses on the Service Lifecycle.

Basic concepts

Before we describe the Service Lifecycle, we need to define some basic concepts.

Good practice

ITIL is presented as a good practice (literally: correct method). This is an approach or method that has proven itself in practice. These good practices can be a solid backing for organizations that want to improve their IT services. In such cases, the best thing to do is to select a generic standard or method that is accessible to everyone, ITIL, COBIT, CMMI, PRINCE2® and ISO/IEC 20000, for example. One of the benefits of these freely accessible generic standards is that they can be applied to several real-life environments and situations. There is also ample training available for open standards. This makes it much easier to train staff.

Another source for good practice is proprietary knowledge. A disadvantage of this kind of knowledge is that it may be customized for the context and needs of a specific organization. Therefore, it may be difficult to adopt or replicate and it may not be as effective in use.

Service

A service is about creating value for the customer. ITIL defines a service as follows:

> A **service** is a means of delivering value to customers by facilitating outcomes the customers want to achieve without the ownership of specific costs or risks.

Outcomes are possible from the performance of tasks, and they are limited by a number of constraints. Services enhance performance and reduce the pressure of constraints. This increases the chances of the desired outcomes being realized.

Value

Value is the core of the service concept. From the customer's perspective value consists of two core components: utility and warranty. Utility is what the customer receives, and warranty is how it is provided.

Service management

ITIL defines service management as follows:

> **Service management** is a set of specialized organizational capabilities for providing value to customers in the form of services.

ITIL discusses some of the fundamental principles of service management that supplement the functions and processes in the ITIL core books. The next principles may help design a service management system:

- **Specialization & coordination** - The goal of service management is to make capabilities and resources available through services that are useful and acceptable to the customer with regard to quality, costs and risks. The service provider takes the weight of responsibility and resource management off the customer's shoulders so that they can focus on the business' core competence. Service management coordinates the business of service management responsibility with regard to certain resources. Utility and warranty act as a guide.
- **Agency principle** - Service management always involves an agent and a principal that seconds this agent to fulfill activities on their behalf. Agents may be consultants, advisors or service providers. Service agents act as intermediary between service providers and customers in conjunction with users. Usually, these agents are the service provider's staff, but they can also be self-service systems and processes for users. Value for the customer is created through agreements between principals and agents.
- **Encapsulation** - The customer's interest focuses on the value of use; he prefers to be spared from any technical details and structure complexity. The "encapsulation principle" is focused on hiding what the customer does not need and showing what is valuable and useful to the customer. Three principles are closely linked to this:
  - separation of concerns
  - modularity: a clear, modular structure
  - loose coupling: reciprocal independence of resources and users

Systems

ITIL describes the organizational structure concepts which proceed from system theory. The Service Lifecycle in ITIL version 3 is a system; however, a function, a process or an organization is a system as well. The definition of a system:

> A **system** is a group of interacting, interrelating, or interdependent components that form a unified whole, operating together for a common purpose.

Feedback and learning are two key aspects in the performance of systems; they turn processes, functions and organizations into dynamic systems. Feedback can lead to learning and growth, not only within a process, but also within an organization in its entirety.

Within a process, for instance, the feedback about the performance of one cycle is, in its turn, input for the next process cycle. Within organizations, there can be feedback between processes, functions and lifecycle phases. Behind this feedback is the common goal: the customer's objectives.

Functions and processes

The distinction between functions and processes is important in ITIL.

What is a function?

> A **function** is a subdivision of an organization that is specialized in fulfilling a specified type of work, and is responsible for specific end results.
> Functions are independent subdivisions with capabilities and resources that are required for their performance and results. They have their own practices and their own knowledge body.

What is a process?

> A **process** is a structured set of activities designed to accomplish a defined objective.
> Processes result in a goal-oriented change, and utilize feedback for self-enhancing and self-corrective actions.

Processes possess the following characteristics:
- They are **measurable** because they are performance-oriented.
- They have **specific results**.
- They provide results to **customers** or stakeholders.
- They **respond to a specific event** - a process is indeed continual and iterative, but is always originating from a certain event.

It can be difficult to determine whether something is a function or a process. According to ITIL, whether it is a function or process depends completely on the organizational design. A good example of a function is a service desk, a good example of a process is change management.

The hierarchical structure of functions can lead to the rise of "silos" in which each function is very self-oriented. This does not benefit the success of the organization as a whole. Processes run through the hierarchical structure of functions; functions often share some processes. This is how processes suppress the rise of functional silos, and help to ensure an improved coordination in between functions.

The Service Lifecycle

ITIL version 3 approaches service management from the lifecycle of a service. The Service Lifecycle is an organization model providing insight into:
- the way service management is structured
- the way the various lifecycle components are linked to each other
- the impact that changes in one component will have on other components and on the entire lifecycle system

So the new ITIL version focuses on the Service Lifecycle, and the way service management components are linked. The processes are also discussed (both the old familiar ones and the new ones) in the cycle phases. They describe how things change.

The Service Lifecycle consists of five phases. Each volume of the new ITIL books describes one of these phases:
- **Service Strategy** - the phase of designing, developing and implementing service management as a strategic resource
- **Service Design** - the design phase of developing appropriate IT services, including architecture, processes, policy and documents; the design goal is to meet the current and future business requirements
- **Service Transition** - the phase of developing and improving capabilities for the transition of new and modified services to production

- **Service Operation** - the phase of achieving effectiveness and efficiency in providing and supporting services in order to ensure value for the customer and the service provider
- **Continual Service Improvement** - the phase of creating and maintaining the value for the customer by design improvement, and service introduction and operation

Service Strategy is the axis of the Service Lifecycle (Figure 2.3) that "runs" all other phases; it is the phase of policymaking and objectives. The phases Service Design, Service Transition and Service Operation implement this strategy, their continual theme is adjustment and change. The Continual Service Improvement phase stands for learning and improving, and embraces all cycle phases. This phase initiates improvement programs and projects, and prioritizes them based on the strategic objectives of the organization.

Figure 2.3 The Service Lifecycle

The Service Lifecycle is a combination of many perspectives on the reality of organizations. This offers more flexibility and control.

The dominant pattern in the Service Lifecycle is the succession of Service Strategy to Service Design, to Service Transition and to Service Operation, and then, through Continual Service Improvement, back to Service Strategy, and so on. The cycle encompasses, however, many patterns. Depending on tasks and responsibilities, a manager can choose his own control perspective. If you are responsible for the design, development or improvement of processes, the best perspective to use is a process perspective. If you are responsible for managing SLAs, contracts and services, the Service Lifecycle perspective and its various phases is likely to meet your needs better.

ITIL Library
The official, new style ITIL Library encompasses the following components:
- Core Library - the five Service Lifecycle publications:
  - Service Strategy
  - Service Design
  - Service Transition
  - Service Operation
  - Continual Service Improvement

  Each book covers a phase from the Service Lifecycle and encompasses various processes. The processes are always described in detail in the book in which they find their key application.
- Complementary portfolio:
  - introduction guide
  - key element guides
  - qualification aids
  - white papers
  - glossary

CHAPTER 3

Lifecycle Phase: Service Transition

3.1 Introduction

This chapter explains how the specifications from Service Design can be effectively converted to a new or changed service.

Objectives

The **goals** of Service Transition include:

- supporting the change process of the business (client)
- reducing variations in the performance and known errors of the new/changed service
- ensuring the service meets the requirements of the service specifications

The **objectives** of Service Transition include:

- the necessary means to realize, plan and manage the new service
- ensuring the minimum impact for the services which are already in production
- improving customer satisfaction and stimulate the proper use of the service and mutual technology

Scope

ITIL defines the **scope** of Service Transition as follows:

> **Service Transition** includes the management and coordination of the processes, systems and functions required for the packaging, building, testing and deployment of a release into production, and establish the service specified in the customer and stakeholder requirements.

A Service Transition generally comprises the following steps:
- planning and preparation
- building and testing
- any pilots
- planning and preparation of the deployment
- deployment and transition
- review and closing of Service Transition

Although change management, service asset and configuration management and knowledge management support all phases of the Service Lifecycle, the ITIL Service Transition book covers these. Release and deployment management, service validation and testing, and evaluation are included in the scope of Service Transition.

Value for the business
An effective Service Transition ensures that the new or changed services are better aligned with the customer's business operation. Specifically:
- the capacity of the business to react quickly and adequately to changes in the market
- changes in the business as a result of takeovers, contracting, etc. are well managed
- more successful changes and releases for the business
- better compliance of business and governing rules
- less deviation between planned budgets and the actual costs
- better insight into the possible risks during and after the input of a service
- higher productivity of customer staff

Optimization
A Service Transition is effective and efficient if the transition delivers what the business requested within the limitations in terms of money and other necessary means. Additionally, it is important that the phase and release plans are coordinated with the business, the service management and the IT strategy.

That is why it matters the extent to which the results of the transition correspond with the specifications of the Service Design: what are the differences between the actual values and those from the specifications? These can influence aspects such as time, money, quality and risks.

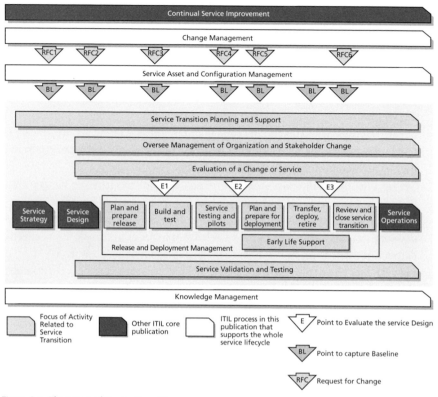

Figure 3.1 The scope of Service Transition

3.2 Basic concepts

The following policies are important for an effective Service Transition and apply to every organization. The approach must still be adjusted to the conditions which differ from organization to organization:

- **Define and implement guidelines and procedures for Service Transition** - Define and document policies for Service Transition. The management team must approve the policies. The management team must pass the policies on to the organization, service providers and partners.
- **Always implement all changes through Service Transition** - All changes in the service portfolio or service catalogue undergo the change management process and the Service Transition phase.
- **Utilize frameworks and standards** - Base Service Transition on generally accepted frameworks, processes and systems. This promotes cooperation between the parties involved in the Service Transition and ensures that they "speak the same language".

- **Re-use of existing processes and systems** - Service Transition processes must be aligned with the processes and systems that the organization already applies. This promotes efficiency and effectiveness. If new processes are developed, re-use is an important design criterion.
- **Align service transition plans with the needs of the business** - Align transition plans, and new or changed services to the requirements and needs of the customer organization.
- **Create relations with stakeholders and maintain these** - During Service Transition, build up a relationship with customer (representatives), users and suppliers, to map their expectations of the new or changed service.
- **Set up effective "controls"** - Set up suitable control mechanisms for the entire lifecycle to guarantee a smooth transition of service changes and releases.
- **Deliver systems for knowledge transfer and decision support** - Service Transition develops systems and processes for knowledge transfer as necessary for an effective delivery of the service, and in order to make decision-making possible.
- **Plan releases and deployment packages** - Release packages must be clear, traceable, clearly planned, designed, built, tested, delivered, distributed and deployed for everyone involved.
- **Anticipate and manage changes in direction** - Ensure that the staff is trained in order to see when "direction adjustments" are necessary during the transition.
- **Manage resources proactively** - Deliver (and manage) shared and specialist resources for the different Service Transition activities in order to avoid delays.
- **Ensure the involvement in an early stage in the Service Lifecycle** - Consult stakeholders in an early stage, so that new or changed services are actually delivering what has been agreed.
- **Assure the quality of a new or changed service** - Verify and validate that the proposed changes can deliver the required service requirements.
- **Proactively improve the quality during a Service Transition** - Proactively plan and improve the quality of a new or changed service.

3.3   Processes and other activities

This section explains the processes and activities of a Service Transition:
- transition planning and support
- change management
- service asset and configuration management
- release and deployment management
- service validation and testing

- evaluation
- service knowledge management

Some of these processes and activities occur in more than one phase of the Service Lifecycle, but are stated in this section as they are central during the Service Transition.

Extensive information about each of these processes can be found in Chapter 5 of this book. The following sections only cover a short summary of the processes.

Transition planning and support

Transition planning and support ensures the planning and coordination of resources in order to realize the specification of the Service Design. Additionally, the process ensures the identification, management and minimization of risks which can interrupt the service during the transition phase.

The scope of transition planning consists of:
- design specifications and requirements of the production department in the transition planning process
- management of:
  - planning
  - support activities
  - transition progress
  - changes
  - issues
  - risks
  - deviations
  - processes
  - supported systems and tools
- monitoring the Service Transition performance
- communication with the client, users and stakeholders

The planning and support activities are:
- set up transition strategy
- prepare Service Transition
- planning and coordination of Service Transition
- support

Change management

The objective of the change management process is to ensure that changes are deployed in a controlled way, evaluated, prioritized, planned, tested, implemented and documented. There can be different reasons for a change such as: cost reduction, service improvement, failure of the service provision or a changed environment.

---

*A **change** is the addition, modification or removal of authorized, planned or supported service or service component and its associated documentation.*

In the change management process it is important to ensure that:
- standardized methods and procedures are used
- all changes are kept in the CMDB
- consideration is given to the risks for the business

Universally the change management activities are comprised of:
- change planning and management
- release planning
- communication
- change authorization
- set up recovery plan
- reporting
- impact assessment
- continual improvement

The specific activities for the management of individual changes are comprised of:
- create and record the Request for Change (RFC)
- review the RFC
- assess and evaluate change
- authorize change
- plan updates
- coordinate change implementation
- review and close change

Service Asset and Configuration Management (SACM)

SACM manages the service assets in order to support the other service management processes.

The objective is: the definition of service and infrastructure components and the maintenance of accurate configuration records. For this it is important that:
- the integrity of the service assets and configuration items (CIs) is protected
- all assets and CIs are categorized in configuration management
- the business and service management processes are effectively supported

SACM may cover non-IT assets and CIs of work products which support the development of services. The scope of the process also includes assets and CIs of other suppliers ("shared assets") in as far as these are important for the service.

The SACM activities are:
- management and planning
- configuration identification
- configuration management (control)
- status accounting and reporting
- verification and audits

Release and deployment management
Release and deployment management is aimed at the building, testing and deploying of the services specified in the Service Design, and ensuring that the client utilizes the service effectively.

The objective of release and deployment management is to ensure that:
- there are release and deployment plans
- release packages (composition) are successfully deployed
- the IT organization transfers knowledge to the clients
- there is minimal disturbance to the services

The process activities of release and deployment management are mainly comprised of:
- planning
- preparation of building, testing and deployment
- building and testing
- service tests and pilots
- planning and preparation for deployment
- transfer, deployment and retirement
- verify deployment
- Early Life Support (ELS)
- review and close

Service validation and testing

Service tests deliver an important contribution to the quality of IT service provision. Tests ensure that the new or changed services are "fit for purpose" and "fit for use".

The goal of service validation and testing is to deliver a service which is of added value to the client's business. When not properly tested, additional incidents, problems and costs occur.

The objectives of service validation and testing are to ensure that:
• the release fulfils the expectation of the client
• the services are "fit for purpose" and "fit for use"
• the specifications (requirements) of the client and other stakeholders are defined

Service validation and testing are applied during the entire Service Lifecycle and are intended to test the quality of the service (parts). Testing directly supports the release and deployment process. The output from testing is used by the evaluation process.

The test process activities are not conducted in a fixed order and can be implemented in parallel. In any case they include:
• validation and test management
• planning and design test
• verification of test plan and design
• preparing the test environment
• testing
• evaluation of exit criteria and reports
• cleaning up and closure

There are many different test techniques and approaches, including: document review, simulation, scenario and laboratory tests, and role plays. The best choice depends on the type of service, the risk profile, the test goal and the test level.

Evaluation

Evaluation is a generic process that is intended to verify whether the performance of "something" is acceptable; for example, whether it has the right price/quality ratio, whether it is continued, whether it is in use, whether it is paid for, and so on.

In the context of Service Transition, the objective of evaluation is the definition of the performance of a service change. Evaluation delivers important input for Continual

Service Improvement (CSI) and future improvement of service development and change management.

The evaluation process is comprised from the following activities:
- planning the evaluation
- evaluation of the predicted performance
- evaluation of the actual performance
- risk management

Knowledge management
The goal of knowledge management is the improvement of the quality of decision-making by ensuring that reliable and secure information is available during the Service Lifecycle. See also the DIKW model in Chapter 5.

The objectives of knowledge management include:
- enabling the service provider to improve the efficiency and quality of the services
- ensuring that the service provider's staff have access to adequate information

Knowledge management is used in the entire lifecycle, but is particularly relevant during the Service Transition: A successful transition depends to a large degree on the information available and knowledge of users, service desk, support and service provider.

Effective sharing of knowledge requires the development and maintenance of a service knowledge management system (SKMS). This system should be available to all information stakeholders and suit all information requirements.

Knowledge management is comprised of the following activities, methods and techniques:
- knowledge management strategy
- knowledge transfer
- data and information management
- the use of the SKMS

Other activities
Communication is central during every Service Transition: the greater the change, the greater the need for communication of the reasons for the change, the possible advantages, the plans for implementation and the effects.

Other operational activities of Service Transition such as the management of organizational changes and the management of stakeholders are explained in the Section "Organization".

3.4 Organization

On the whole, the activities of a process are not carried out by a single department. The different activities, for example of SACM, are carried out by departments such as service operation, application management, network management and system management. Therefore, the process activities are related to the different IT departments and their respective staff. Roles and responsibilities are also defined.

Generic roles

Process owner - The process owner ensures that all process activities are carried out and:
- is responsible for the process strategy, and assists in the design
- provides process documentation, guidelines and procedures and their application
- ensures there are adequate resources

Service owner - The service owner holds the responsibility, toward the client, for the initiation, transition and maintenance of a service and:
- is the contact person and ensures that the service meets the requirements
- identifies improvement points and provides data and reports for service monitoring
- is accountable for the delivery of the service to IT Management

Organizational context

The interfaces of other departments and third parties in Service Transition must be clearly defined and known. Programs, projects, Service Design and service provider all contribute towards the Service Transition.

Service Transition is actively managed by a **service transition manager**. The Service Transition manager is responsible for the daily management and control of the Service Transition teams and their activities. An example of a Service Transition organization is presented in Figure 3.2.

Service Transition roles and responsibilities

This section describes a number of roles and responsibilities within Service Transition, although some roles also fall within other lifecycle phases. Depending on the size of the organization and the scope of the service which is changed, some of these roles can be carried out by one person.

The responsibilities of the **service asset manager** include:
- formulating process objectives and implementing the policy, the process standards, plans and procedures
- evaluating the existing asset management systems and implementing the new systems
- indicating the scope and function of the process, which items must be managed and the information that must be established
- taking care of communication about the process and making it known
- taking care of resources and training
- setting up the identification and the naming conventions of assets
- taking care of the evaluation of the use of tooling
- setting up interfaces with other processes
- planning the completion of the asset database
- making reports
- assisting with audits and taking care of corrective actions

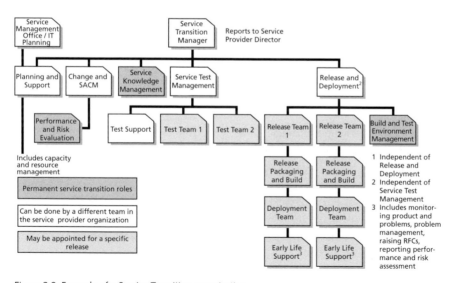

Figure 3.2 Example of a Service Transition organization

The responsibilities of the **configuration manager** include:
- formulating process objectives and implementing the policy, the process standards, plans and procedures
- evaluating the existing configuration management systems and implementing the new systems
- indicating the scope and function of the process, which items must be managed and the information that must be established
- taking care of communication about the process and making it known
- taking care of resources and training
- setting up the identification and the naming conventions of CIs
- taking care of the evaluation of the use of tooling
- setting up interfaces with other processes
- evaluating existing CMS systems and implementation of new systems
- planning the filling in of CMS in the CMDBs
- making reports
- assisting with audits and taking corrective actions

The **change manager** has responsibilities (some of which can be delegated) including:
- receiving, logging and prioritizing (in collaboration with the initiator) RFCs, rejecting RFS based on the criteria
- preparing and chairing CAB and ECAB meetings
- deciding who attends which meeting, who receives RFCs, what must be changed there
- publishing Changes Schedules (SCs)
- maintaining change logs
- closing RFCs
- reviewing implemented changes
- making reports

The **Change Advisory Board (CAB)** is an advisory consultation body. The specific roles and responsibilities of the CAB will be explained in Section 5.2.

The responsibilities of the **release packaging and build manager** include:
- final release configuration
- building the final release and testing it (prior to independent testing)
- reporting known faults and workarounds
- input to the final implementation sign-off

The **deployment manager** is responsible for the following including:
- the final service implementation
- coordination of all release documentation, release notes and communication
- planning of the deployment, in combination with change management, knowledge management and SACM
- providing guidance during the release process
- giving feedback concerning the effectiveness of a release
- recording metrics for deployment to ensure within agreed SLAs

ITIL recognizes the following roles in the Service Transition phase of the Service Lifecycle, but this falls outside the scope of this book and the ITIL Foundations exams:
- configuration analyst
- configuration manager
- CMS manager
- configuration management team
- change authority
- risk-evaluation manager
- service knowledge manager
- test support
- Early Life Support (ELS)
- building and test environment management

Organizational change management

Significant change of a service also means a change of the organization. This can vary from "the transfer of a staff member to another department" to large changes such as "the manner of working in the organization". For example: a mail order company no longer sells its products by a printed catalogue but via a website.

The following aspects are important in organizational change management:
- **The emotional change cycle** - One of the biggest causes of failure of changes is not sufficiently considering the way in which the changes affect people. Therefore consider the emotional phases that people can experience before accepting changes. The emotional phases are: shock, avoidance, external blame, self blame and acceptance.
- **The role of Service Transition in organizational changes** - The management of change is the responsibility of the managers and heads of department involved in this specific change. However, the Service Transition manager or process owner is an

important party in the change, and therefore Service Transition plays an important role in organizational changes. Service Transition must:

- show awareness of the different cultures at organizational and individual levels
- include active participation in the changing of people's attitudes (who are active within the lifecycle)
- support individuals in such a way that the implementation of changes is consistently executed
- evaluate whether the IT organization is sufficiently capable
- guarantee that the change is accepted by the majority in their daily work method
- take care to ensure that knowledge transfer, training, team building, process improvement and evaluation of staff are sufficiently competent

• **Planning and implementation of organizational changes** - In the planning and design of changes there is often insufficient consideration for the organizational side and the people. The focus lies on the technical aspect of the change. That is why it is important that the project plans also state the organizational changes caused by the change.

• **Products** - Service Strategy and Service Design result in several work products which support the management of organizational changes during the Service Transition, for example:

- stakeholder analysis
- organizational and competency assessments
- service management process models
- guidelines for processes and procedures
- communication plan
- RACI matrix (Responsible, Accountable, Consulted, Informed)

• **Evaluation of readiness for organizational change** - It is good practice to make a checklist to assess if the organization fulfills the requirements for transition in terms of roles and skills.

• **Monitoring of progress** - Research and surveys must be carried out on a regular basis at different levels in the organization concerning the effectiveness and the success of a Service Transition program. Use the result of the research to define how much progress is achieved with the transition. It will also indicate to staff that they are being heard and that their input is important in the transition.

• **Manage organizational changes in sourcing** - Sourcing IT services is one of the most serious organizational changes. There are many consequences for the personnel which must be considered and carefully prepared, such as:
the shock for staff

- changes in the way in which the business and the service provider do business with each other
- change of location with all the associated risks
- **Methods and techniques for organizational changes** - Numerous methods, techniques and best practices exist for management of changes, such as J.P. Kotter's "Changes in eight steps" and Rosabeth Moss Kanter's theory about the reasons why people resist change. It is important to make the best possible use of these.

Stakeholder management

Stakeholder management is a crucial success factor in Service Transition. This is why a strategy should be developed in the Service Design phase. Explain:
- who the stakeholders are
- what their interest are
- what their influence is
- how they are included in the project or program
- what information is shared with them

A stakeholder map is a useful tool to map the different interest of the stakeholders. (See Figure 3.3.)

Stakeholders	Strategic direction	Financial	Operational changes	Interface with customers	Public safety	Competitive position
Business partner	●	●		●		●
Project teams			●			
Customers		●		●	●	
Press and media						●
Trade unions			●			
Staff	●		●			
Regulatory bodies		●			●	

Figure 3.3 Stakeholder matrix

Further a **stakeholder analysis** assists in finding out what the requirements and interests of the stakeholders are, and what their final influence and power will be during the transition.

Finally, the turnover of stakeholders during the Service Lifecycle must also be considered.

3.5   Methods, technology and tools

Technology plays an important part in the support of Service Transition. It can be divided into two types:
- **IT service management systems:**
  - enterprise frameworks which offer integration capabilities to integrate and link in the CMDB or other tools
  - system, network and application management tools
  - service dashboards and reporting tools
- **Specific ITSM technology and tools:**
  - service knowledge management systems
  - collaboration tools, content management systems and workflow tools
  - tools for data mining, data extraction and data transformation
  - tools for measuring and reporting
  - test (management) tools
  - publication tools
  - release and deployment technology

In addition specialized tools are available for change management, configuration management and release management, such as:
- configuration management systems
- tools for version control
- document management systems
- design tools
- distribution and installation tools
- construction and deployment tools

A more elaborate description of the various tools for Service Transition and the underlying processes is beyond the scope of this book.

3.6 Implementation

The implementation of Service Transition in a "greenfield" situation (from zero) is only feasible when establishing a new service provider. Most service providers focus on the improvement of the Service Transition (processes). For the improvement of Service Transition (processes) the following five aspects are important:

1. **Justification** - The benefits of effective Service Transition are not always immediately visible to the client. Gathering evidence of the damage caused by an ineffective transition phase can justify the establishment or improvement of Service Transition. Take into consideration aspects such as: the costs of failed changes or errors in services in the production environment which could have been avoided if a good test process had been used.

2. **Design** - Factors to take into account when designing Service Transition are:
   - standards and guidelines to which the design must adhere
   - relationships with other supporting services (HRM, telecommunications, facilities management), project and program management, clients, end users and other stakeholders
   - budget and means

3. **Introduction** - Experience has taught us that it is unwise to apply the improved or newly implemented (and therefore unproven) Service Transition to current projects. In all likelihood the advantages do not outweigh the disadvantages resulting from the disruption of the project.

4. **Cultural aspects** - Even formalizing existing procedures will lead to cultural changes in an organization. Take this into consideration and do not only think of those staff that are directly involved in the Service Transition, but consider all stakeholders.

5. **Risks and advantages** - Do not make any decisions about the introduction or improvement of Service Transition without an insight into the risks and advantages to expect.

Relationships with other lifecycle phases

Even though this book presents Service Transition as a more or less delimited lifecycle phase, this does not mean that it can be viewed on its own. Without the input from Service Design and the output to Service Operation, Service Transition has no purpose.

There is also the input and output of knowledge and experience from and to Service Transition. This flow of knowledge and experience works both ways:

- **Against the flow** - For instance Service Operation shares practical experiences with Service Transition as to how similar services behave in the production environment. Experiences from Service Transition supply input for the assessment of the designs from Service Design.

- **With the flow** - Service Design supplies Service Transition with the knowledge needed to implement a change (for instance the different designs), and Service Transition supplies production experiences (for instance from testing) which could prove to be important for the daily management of the service.

Figure 3.4. Flow of knowledge and experience from and to other lifecycle phases

Challenges and critical success factors

For a successful Service Transition, several challenges need to be conquered, such as:
- taking into account all stakeholders (and their different perspectives) and maintaining relationships which could be important within Service Transition
- the lack of harmonization and integration of processes and disciplines which influence Service Transition
- finding the balance between a stable operation environment and being able to respond to changing business requirements in a flexible manner
- finding the balance between pragmatism and bureaucracy
- creating an environment in which standardization and knowledge sharing is stimulated
- creating a culture in which one is responsive to cooperation and cultural changes
- ensuring that the quality of services corresponds to the quality of the business
- finding the balance between "taking risks" and "avoiding risks"; this balance must correspond to that of the business
- the integration with other lifecycle phases, processes and disciplines
- a clear definition of the roles and responsibilities
- having the correct tools for managing the IT infrastructure
- developing good quality systems, tools, processes, procedures for Service Transition

Risks

Potential risks of Service Transition are:
- de-motivation of staff as a result of changed responsibilities and roles
- unforeseen expenses
- resistance to change
- lack of knowledge sharing
- poor integration between processes
- lack of maturity and integration of systems and tools

Finally, there can be circumstances in which Service Transition can have additional risk, for instance as a result of a lack of money or resources, or political problems.

CHAPTER 4

Introduction to Functions and Processes

4.1 Introduction

Processes are *internal* affairs for the IT service provider. An organization that is still trying to gain control of its processes therefore has an **internal focus**. Organizations that focus on gaining control of their systems in order to provide services are still internally focused. The organization is not ready for an **external focus** until it controls its services and is able to vary them on request. This external focus is required to evolve into that desirable customer-focused organization.

Because organizations can be in different stages of maturity, IT managers require a broad orientation in their discipline. Most organizations are now working on the introduction of a process-focused or customer-focused approach, or still have to start working on this. Process control is therefore a vital step on the road towards a **mature customer-focused organization**.

ITIL has made an important contribution to the organization of that process-focused operating method in the past decade. The development started in North-western Europe and has made some progress on most other continents in the last few years also. On a global scale, however, a minimal number of organizations have actually started with this approach - and an even smaller number have made serious progress at this point. The organization change projects that were thought to be necessary to convert to a process-focused organization were not all successful.

These findings lead us to conclude that the majority of organizations in the world require access to good information and best practices concerning the **business processes of**

IT organizations. Fortunately, that information is abundant. The ITIL version 2 books provide comprehensive documentation on the most important processes, while ITIL version 3 adds even more information.

The **process model** is at least as important as the processes because processes must be deployed in the right relationships to achieve the desired effect of a process-focused approach. There are many different process models available. The experiences gained with these processes and process models in recent years have been documented comprehensively in books, magazines and white papers, and have been presented at countless conventions.

4.2 Management of processes

Every organization aims to realize its vision, mission, strategy, objectives and policies, which means that appropriate activities have to be undertaken.

For example, a restaurant will have to purchase fresh ingredients, the chefs will have to work together to provide consistent results, and there should be no major differences in style among the waiting staff. A restaurant will only be awarded a three-star rating when it manages to provide the same high quality over an extended period of time. This is not always the case: there will be changes among the waiting staff, a successful approach may not last, and chefs often leave to open their own restaurants. Providing consistently high quality means that the component activities have to be coordinated: the better and more efficiently the kitchen operates, the higher the quality of service that can be provided to the guests.

In the example of the restaurant, appropriate activities include buying vegetables, bookkeeping, ordering publicity material, receiving guests, cleaning tables, peeling potatoes and making coffee. With just such an unstructured list, something will be left out and staff will easily become confused. It is therefore a better idea to structure the activities. Preferably these will be structured in such a way as to allow us to see how each group of activities contributes to the objectives of the business, and how they are related to other activities.

Such groups of activities are known as **processes**. If the process structure of an organization is clearly described, it will show:
- what has to be done
- what the expected inputs and results are
- how we measure whether the processes deliver the expected results
- how the results of one process affect those of another process

Processes can be defined in many ways. Depending upon the objectives of the creator, more or less emphasis will be on specific aspects. For example, a highly detailed process description will allow for a high level of control. Superficial process definitions will illustrate that the creator does not care much about the way in which the steps are executed.

Once the processes are defined, the roles, responsibilities and people can be assigned to specific aspects, bringing the process to the level of a *procedure*.

Processes

When arranging activities into processes, we do not use the existing allocation of tasks, nor the existing departmental divisions. This is a conscious choice. By opting for a process structure, it often becomes evident that certain activities in the organization are uncoordinated, duplicated, neglected or unnecessary.

> A **process** is a structured set of activities designed to accomplish a defined objective.

Instead, we look at the **objective** of the process and the **relationships** with other processes. A process is a series of activities carried out to convert input into an output, and ultimately into an outcome. The **input** is concerned with the resources being used in the process. The (reported) **output** describes the immediate results of the process, while the **outcome** indicates the long-term results of the process (in terms of meaningful effect). Through **control** activities, we can associate the input and output of each of the processes with **policies and standards** to provide information about the results to be obtained by the process. Control regulates the input and the **throughput** in case the throughput or output parameters are not compliant with these standards and policies. This produces chains of processes that show the input that goes into the organization and what the result, and it also monitors points in the chains in order to check the quality of the products and services provided by the organization.

The standards for the output of each process have to be defined, in such a way that the complete chain of processes in the process model meets the corporate objective. If the output of a process meets the defined requirements, then the process is **effective** in transforming its input into its output. To be really effective, the outcome should be taken into consideration rather than merely focusing on the output. If the activities in the process are also carried out with the minimum required effort and cost, then the process is **efficient**. It is the task of process management to use **planning and control** to ensure that processes are executed in an effective and efficient way.

We can study each process separately to optimize its quality. The **process owner** is responsible for the process results. The **process manager** is responsible for the realization and structure of the process, and reports to the process owner.

The logical combination of activities results in clear transfer points where the quality of processes can be monitored. In the restaurant example, we can separate responsibility for purchasing and cooking, so that the chefs do not have to purchase anything and can concentrate on their core activities.

The management of the organization can provide control on the basis of the process quality of the process as demonstrated by data from the results of each process. In most cases, the relevant **performance indicators** and standards will already be agreed upon. In this case the process manager can do the day-to-day control of the process. The process owner will assess the results based on a **report** of performance indicators and checks whether the results meet the agreed standard. Without clear indicators, it would be difficult for a process owner to determine whether the process is under control, and if planned improvements are being implemented.

Processes are often described using **procedures** and **work instructions**.

> A **procedure** is a specified way to carry out an activity or a process.
> A procedure describes the "how", and can also describe "who" carries the activities out. A procedure may include stages from different processes. A procedure can vary depending on the organization.
>
> A set of **work instructions** defines how one or more activities in a procedure should be carried out in detail, using technology or other resources.

A process is defined as a logically related series of activities executed to meet the goals of a defined objective. Processes are composed of two kinds of activities: the activities to realize the goal (operational activities concerned with the throughput), and the activities to manage these (control activities). The control activities make sure the operational activities (the workflow) are performed in time, in the right order, etc. (For example, in the processing of changes it is always ensured that a test is performed *before* a release is taken into production and not *afterwards*.)

Processes and departments

Most businesses are hierarchically organized. There are departments that are responsible for the activities of a group of employees. There are various ways of structuring departments, such as by customer, product, region or discipline. IT services generally depend on several departments, customers or disciplines. For example, if there is an IT service to provide users with access to an accounting program on a central computer, this will involve several disciplines. The computer center has to make the program and database accessible, the data and telecommunications department has to make the computer center accessible, and the PC support team has to provide users with an interface to access the application.

Processes that span several departments (teams) can monitor the quality of a service by monitoring particular aspects of quality, such as availability, capacity, cost and stability. A service organization will try to match these quality aspects with the customer's demands. The structure of such processes can ensure that good information is available about the provision of services, so that the planning and control of services can be improved.

Figure 4.1 shows a basic example of the combinations of activities in a process (indicated by the dashed lines).

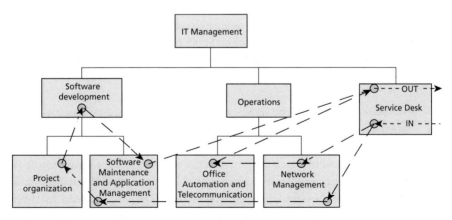

Figure 4.1 Processes and departments

IT service management and processes

IT service management has been known as the process and service-focused approach of what was initially known as Information Technology management. The shift of management from infrastructure to processes has paved the way for the term IT service management as a process and customer-focused discipline. Processes should always have a defined objective. The objective of IT service management processes is to contribute to the quality of the IT services. Quality management and process control are part of the organization and its policies.

By using a process approach, best practices for IT service management describe how services can be delivered, using the most effective and efficient series of activities. The Service Lifecycle in ITIL V3 is based on these process descriptions. The structure and allocation of tasks and responsibilities between functions and departments depends on the type of organization, and these structures vary widely among IT departments, and they often change. The description of the process structure however, provides a common point of reference that changes less rapidly. This can help to maintain the quality of IT services during and after reorganizations, and also among service providers and partners as they change. This makes service providers far less sensitive to organizational change, and much more flexible: providers can continually adapt their organization to changing conditions, leaving the core of their processes in place. In this way the shop can stay open during reconstruction work. However, reality may pose some practical problems, making this more difficult in practice than it seems in theory.

Applying the best process definitions of the industry allows IT service providers to concentrate on their business. As with other fields of industry, the processes in the IT industry are similar for all organizations of the same nature. Many of the process descriptions documented in ITIL have been recognized as the best that the industry could hope to adopt.

4.3 Teams, roles and positions in ITSM

Organizations divide the various tasks for carrying out processes or activities in many different ways. Tasks can be covered by organizational bodies, such as groups, teams, departments or divisions. These organizational bodies are then managed in **hierarchical organizations** by a line manager, who has a certain "span of control" and who manages one or more of these bodies. **Flat organizations** have relatively few layers in this hierarchy. Organizations can also divide the tasks more in the spirit of equality, such as, for example, **network organizations**, in which the cooperation between the various bodies is paramount.

Besides hierarchical organizations, which manage through "the line", there are also **project organizations**, which manage primarily by using temporary forms of project cooperation, while **process organizations** are managed primarily by means of an agreed work method. Obviously, these types of management can be combined in innumerable ways. As a result of this, we are seeing a great number of unique organizational configurations in the field.

Organizations can distinguish themselves from other organizations, particularly in respect to the type of organization they operate. An organization that is directed toward hierarchy will have a staff primarily of senior line management. A process-oriented organization will have staff that are responsible for processes. Depending on the degree to which management is based on processes, the line or projects, the staff will consist of a mix of the relevant responsible managers.

When setting up an organization, positions and roles are also used, in addition to the various groups (teams, departments, divisions). **Roles** are sets of responsibilities, activities and authorities granted to a person or team. One person or team may have multiple roles; for example, the roles of Configuration Manager and Change Manager may be carried out by a single person. **Positions** (functions) are traditionally recognized as tasks and responsibilities that are assigned to a specific person. A person in a particular position has a clearly defined package of tasks and responsibilities which may include various roles. Positions can also be more broadly defined as a logical concept that refers to the people and automated measures that carry out a clearly defined process, an activity or a combination of processes or activities.

4.4 Tools used in ITSM

In the performance of tasks in IT service management, innumerable automated support aids can be used: these are referred to as tools. With the help of these tools, management tasks can be automated; for example, monitoring tasks or software distribution tasks. Other tools support the performance of the activities themselves; for example, service desk tools or service management tools. The latter category, in fact, supports the management of several processes and are therefore often referred to as workflow tools - although they may not have actual workflow engines.

The fact that the IT field is fundamentally focused on automated facilities (for information processing) has led to a virtual deluge of tools appearing on the market, which have greatly increased the performance capacity of IT organizations.

4.5 Communication in IT service organizations

People, process, partners and technology provide the main "machinery" of any organization, but they only work well if the machine is oiled: **communication** is an essential element in any organization. If the people do not know about the processes or use the wrong instructions or tools, the output may not be as anticipated.

People are core assets of the organization. This is not only due to the fact that they need to be in place to perform certain activities or to take decisions, but also because people have the good habit of communicating. When an organization applies highly detailed instructions for all its activities, it will end up in a bureaucracy. On the other hand, an organization without any rules is will most likely end up in chaos. Whichever balance an organization is trying to find here, it will always benefit enormously from communication between the people in the organization. A regular and formal meeting culture will support this, but organizations should not underestimate the important role of informal communication: many projects have been saved by means of a simple chat in the tea room, or in the car park.

Formal structures on communication include:
*   **reporting** - internal and external reporting, aimed at management or customers, project progress reports, alerts
*   **meetings** - formal project meetings, regular meetings with specific targets
*   **online facilities** - email systems, chat-rooms, pagers, groupware, document sharing systems, messenger facilities, teleconferencing and virtual meeting facilities
*   **notice boards** - near the coffee maker, water cooler, at the entrance of the building, in the company restaurant

IT teams and departments, as well as users, internal customers and service production teams, must communicate with each other. The **stakeholders** for communication can thus be found among all managers and employees who are involved in service management, in all the layers of the organization, and with all customers, users and service providers. Good communication can prevent problems. All communication must have a particular goal or result. Every team, process and every department must have a clear **communications policy**.

IT service management includes several types of communication, such as:
*   routine operational communication
*   communication between teams
*   performance reports
*   communication during projects

- communication when there are changes
- communication in case of exceptions
- communication in case of emergencies
- training for new or adapted processes and service designs
- communication with service production teams regarding service strategies and design

4.6 Culture

Organizations that want to change, for example to improve the quality of their services, will eventually be confronted with the current organizational culture and will have to deal with any changes to this culture as a consequence of the overall change. The organizational culture, or corporate culture, refers to the way in which people deal with each other in the organization; the way in which decisions are made and implemented; and the attitude of employees to their work, customers, service providers, superiors and colleagues.

Culture, which depends on the standards and values of the people in the organization, cannot be controlled, but it can be influenced. Influencing the culture of an organization requires leadership in the form of a clear and consistent policy, as well as a supportive personnel policy.

The corporate culture can have a major influence on the provision of IT services. Businesses value innovation in different ways. In a stable organization, where the culture places little value on innovation, it will be difficult to adjust its IT services in line with changes in the organization of the customer. If the IT department is unstable, then a culture which values change can pose a serious threat to the quality of its services. In that case, a "free for all" culture can develop where many uncontrolled changes lead to a large number of faults.

4.7 Processes, projects, programs and portfolios

Activities can be managed from a process perspective, from an organizational hierarchy (line) perspective, from a project perspective, or from any combination of these three. Organizations that tend to apply just one of these management systems often miss the benefits of the others. The practical choice often depends upon history, culture, available skills and competences, and personal preferences. The optimum choice may be entirely different, but the requirements for applying this optimum may be hard to realize and vary in time.

There are no "hard and fast laws" for the way an organization should combine processes, projects and programs. However, it is generally accepted that there are some consequences attached to modern practices in IT service organizations, since the most widely accepted approach to service management is based on process management. This means that whenever the organization works with projects or programs, it should have established how these approaches work together.

The practical relationship between projects and processes is determined by the relative position of both in terms of "leading principles for the management of the organization": if projects are considered more important than processes, then decisions on projects will overrule decisions on processes; as a consequence, the organization will not be able to implement a stable set of processes. If it is the other way around, with projects only able to run within the constraints of agreed processes, then project management will be a discipline that will have to adapt to new boundaries and definitions (e.g. since projects always change something from A to B, they will most likely fall under the regime of Change, Release and Deployment Management).

The most suitable solution is dependent upon the understanding of the role of IT service management in the organization. To be able to find a solution for this management challenge, it is recommended that a common understanding of processes, projects, programs, and even portfolio's is created. The following definitions may be used:
- **Process** - A process is a structured set of activities designed to accomplish a defined objective.
- **Project** - A project is a temporary organization, with people and other assets required to achieve an objective.
- **Program** - A program consists of a number of projects and activities that are planned and managed together to achieve an overall set of related objectives.
- **Portfolio** - A portfolio is a set of projects and/or programs, which are not necessarily related, brought together for the sake of control, coordination and optimization of the portfolio in its totality. NB: In ITIL, a service portfolio is the complete set of services that are managed by a service provider.

Since the project/program/portfolio grouping is a hierarchical set of essential project resources, the issue can be downscaled to that of a relationship between a project and a process.

The most elementary difference between a process and a project is the one-off character of a project, versus the continuous character of the process. If a project has achieved its objectives, it means the end of the project. Processes can be run many times, both in parallel and in sequence. The nature of a process is aimed at its repeatable character:

processes are defined only in case of a repeatable string of activities that are important enough to be standardized and optimized.

Projects are aimed at changing a situation A into a situation B. This can involve a simple string of activities, but it can also be a very complex series of activities. Other elements of importance for projects include money, time, quality, organization and information. Project structures are normally used only if at least one of these elements is of considerable value.

Actually, projects are just ways of organizing a specific change in a situation. In that respect they have a resemblance with processes. It is often a matter of focus: processes focus at the specific sequence of activities, the decisions taken at certain milestone stages, and the quality of the activities involved. Processes are continuously instantiated and repeated, and use the same approach each time. Projects focus more at the time and money constraints, in terms of resources spent on the change and the projects end, and projects vary much more than processes.

A very practical way of combining the benefits of both management systems might be as follows:

- Processes set the scene for how specific series of activities are performed.
- Projects can be used to transform situation A into situation B, and always refer to a change.
- If the resources (time, money, or other) involved in a specific process require the level of attention that is normally applied in a project, then (part of) the process activities can be performed as a project, but always under the control of the process: if changes are performed, using project management techniques, the agreed change management policies still apply.

This would allow organizations to maintain a continuous customer focus and apply a process approach to optimize this customer focus, and at the same time benefit from the high level of resource control that can be achieved when using project management techniques.

4.8 Functions and processes in the lifecycle phases

For the sake of readability and uniformity, the following structure for the descriptions was used as much as possible:

- **introduction** - describes the purpose and aims of the process or function, its scope, value to the business, principles, guidelines, starting points and basic concepts

- **activities, methods and techniques** - explains the process or function in greater detail based on the workflow of activities (if possible); also describes commonly used methods and techniques
- **interfaces** - describes how the process or function is triggered, its inputs and outputs, and its links to other functions and processes
- **metrics** - describes the process metrics, in particular the Key Performance Indicators (KPIs)
- **implementation** - describes the Critical Success Factors (CSFs), challenges, risks and traps that may apply for the introduction of a process or function

Functions and Processes in Service Transition

5.1 Transition Planning and Support

Introduction

The **goals** for transition planning and support include:

- planning and coordinating resources in order to ensure that the specifications of the Service Design are realized
- starting with the transition phase, identify, manage and limit risks that could interrupt the service

The **objectives** for transition planning and support include:

- plan and coordinate people and means within the frameworks
- make sure that everyone applies the same frameworks and standards
- report service issues
- provide clear and extensive plans
- support transition teams and others involved
- controlled planning of changes
- report issues, risks and other deviations

Scope

The following activities are included in the scope of transition planning:

- include design specifications and product requirements in the transition plans
- manage:
  - plans
  - supporting activities

- transition progress
- changes
- issues
- risks
- deviations
- processes
- supporting systems and tools
- monitor Service Transition achievements
- communicate with clients, users and stakeholders

Value for the business
An integrated approach to planning improves the alignment of transition plans with the customer, service provider, business and change project plans.

Basic concepts
The **Service Design Package** (**SDP**) contains the following information required by the service transition team:
- applicable service packages (e.g. core service package, service level package)
- service specifications
- service models
- architectural design required to deliver the new of changed service including constraints
- definition and design of each release package
- detailed design of how the components will be assembled and integrated into a release package
- release and deployment plans
- service acceptance criteria

In the **release guidelines and policy**, the following subjects are addressed:
- naming conventions, distinguishing release types, such as: **major release, minor release** and **emergency release**
- roles and responsibilities; many people from different organizations can be involved with a release; it is useful to set up a responsibility matrix for this purpose
- release frequency, the expected frequency of each type of release
- approach for accepting and grouping changes in to a release
- how the configuration baseline for the release is captured and verified against the actual release contents e.g. hardware, software, documentation and knowledge

- entry and exit criteria and authority for acceptance of the release into each Service Transition stage and into the controlled test, training, disaster recovery and production environments
- the criteria authorization for leaving Early Life Support (ELS) and handover to service operations

Activities, methods and techniques

The activities for planning and support consist of:

1. set up transition strategy
2. prepare Service Transition
3. plan and coordinate Service Transition
4. support

1. Set up transition strategy

The transition strategy defines the overall approach to organizing Service Transition and allocating resources. Aspects that may be addressed in the transition strategy are:

- purpose, goals and objectives
- context and scope
- applicable standards, agreements, legal, regulatory and contractual agreements
- organizations and stakeholders involved in the Service Transition
- framework for Service Transition
- criteria for success and failure
- people; roles and responsibilities
- approach including transition model, plans for managing changes, assets, configurations and knowledge; transition estimation; preparation; evaluation; error handling; KPIs
- the products (deliverables) that are the result of the transition activities such as transition plans, schedule of milestones, financial requirements

The SDP defines the various phases of the Service Transition. These may consist of: acquiring and testing components, testing service release, Service Operation ready test, rollout, ELS, review and close service transition.

2. Prepare Service Transition

Preparatory activities consist of:

- review and acceptance of inputs from other Service Lifecycle phases review and check the input deliverables e.g. SDP, Service Acceptance Criteria (SAC) and evaluation report
- identifying, raising and scheduling RFCs

- checking the configuration baselines are recorded in configuration management before the start of service transition
- checking transition readiness

3. Plan and coordinate Service Transition

A **service transition plan** describes the tasks and activities required to release and deploy a release into the test environments and into production including

- work environment and infrastructure
- schedule of milestones
- activities and tasks to be performed
- staffing, resource requirements, budgets and timescales at each stage
- lead times and contingency

Good **integrated planning** and management are essential to deploy a release across distributed environments and locations into production successfully An **integrated set of transition plans** should be maintained that are linked to lower level plans such as release, build and test plans.

It is *best practice* to manage several releases in a **program**, with each significant deployment run as a **project**.

Implement **quality reviews** for all Service Transition, release and deployment plans. Questions that might be asked are:

- Are the service transition plans and release plans up-to-date, authorized and are the release dates known?
- Were any risks related to impact on costs, organization and technology taken into account?
- Are new configuration items (CIs) compatible with each other and with configuration items in the target environment?
- Are the people who need to work with it sufficiently trained?
- Have potential changes in the business environment been taken into account?

4. Transition process support

Service Transition advises and **supports** all stakeholders. The planning and support team will provide insight for the stakeholders regarding Service Transition processes and supporting systems and tools. In addition, the team will perform **management/ administration** of changes, work orders, issues, risks, communication and deployment. The team will also update stakeholders regarding planning and process.

Finally, Service Transition activities are **monitored**: the implementation of activities is compared with the way they were intended (as formulated in the transition plan and model).

Interfaces

The **trigger** for service transition is an approved (authorized) RFC. **Inputs** for Transition planning include:
- authorized RFCs
- SDP
- definition of the release package and design specifications
- SAC

Outputs for transition planning include:
- transition strategy
- integral collection of Service Transition plans

Metrics

The most important **KPIs** for transition planning and support are:
- the number of implemented releases that met the customers agreed requirements
- decrease in the number of deviations with respect to intended scope, quality, costs and resources
- increased customer and user satisfaction regarding plans and communication
- decrease in the number of issues, risks and delays as a result of improved planning

5.2   Change Management

Introduction

Changes have a proactive or reactive **reason**. Examples of a proactive reason are cost reduction or service improvement. Examples of reactive changes are solving service disruptions or adapting the service to a changing environment.

Changes must be **controlled** adequately, so that:
- exposure to risks is minimized
- the severity of the impact and service interruption is minimized
- the change is implemented successfully on first attempt

The **goals** of change management are:
- respond to the customer's changing business
- responding to Requests for Change (RFCs) from the business and IT

The **objective** of the change management process is ensuring that changes are recorded, assessed, authorized, prioritized, planned, tested, implemented and documented and reviewed in a controlled manner.

The change management process must:
- use standardized methods and procedures
- record all changes in the CMDB
- take account of risks for the business

Scope
The ITIL definition of a change is:

> A **change** is the addition, modification or removal of authorized, planned or supported service or service component and its associated documentation.

The scope of service management covers changes to baselined service assets and CIs across the whole Service Lifecycle. The Section "Service asset and configuration management" later in this chapter discusses these issues in greater detail.

Every organization must itself define which changes its change management process does and does not cover. For instance, changing a defective hard drive of a pc may not be part of the change management process.

Figure 5.1 shows the scope of the change management process as well as the interfaces of the process with the business at the strategic, tactical and operational levels.

Figure 5.1 Scope of change management

Value for the business
Service and infrastructure changes can have a negative impact on the business through service disruption and delay in identifying business requirements, but change management enables the service providers to add value to the business.

For example:
- changes relating to financial regulations, such as SOX, or other rules of good governance
- timely implementation of changes so that the business' deadlines are achieved
- reducing the number of failed changes, thereby reducing the number of service interruptions
- prioritizing changes and responding adequately to change requests from the customer
- reducing the mean time to restore services (MTRS)

Thanks to the increased dependency on IT services, and because the underlying information technology has become so complex, significant efficiency benefits can be realized by means of well structured and planned changes and releases. Some indicators of inadequate change management are:

- unauthorized changes
- unplanned downtime
- implemented changes with little success
- high number of "emergency changes"
- delayed project implementations

Policies

Policies for supporting change management are:

- creating a zero tolerance culture in relation to unauthorized changes
- aligning the change management process with other change processes in the organization
- effective prioritization, e.g. innovative versus preventive versus detective versus corrective changes
- establishing accountability and responsibilities for changes through the lifecycle
- establishing a single focal point for changes
- ensuring integration with other service management processes
- setting up "change windows", performance and risk assessments, performance measures

Design and planning

The change management process is planned in combination with release and configuration management. This makes it possible to assess the impact of changes on services and releases.

The requirement and design for the change management processes include:

- requirements relating to relevant laws and regulations
- an approach to eliminate unauthorized changes
- identification and classification
- organization, roles, responsibilities
- stakeholders
- grouping and relating changes
- procedures
- interfaces with other service management processes

Basic concepts

A **Request for Change (RFC)** is a formal request to change one or more CIs.

A **standard change** is a change of a service or infrastructure component that change management must register, but is of low risk and is pre-authorized. These are routine changes, such as PC upgrades.

An **emergency change** is intended to repair a failure (ASAP) in an IT service that has a large negative impact on the business. If this requires permission from the CAB, but the full CAB cannot be convened, it is necessary to identify a smaller organization to make emergency decisions: the **Emergency CAB (ECAB)**.

An emergency change, too, must be tested and documented to the greatest possible extent.

The **Change Advisory Board (CAB)** is a consultation body that meets at fixed intervals to assess changes and help change management prioritize the changes. It may include representatives from all key stakeholders and departments, including:
- customers
- end users
- application developers
- system administrators
- experts
- service desk representatives
- production
- service provider representatives

The CAB must have a number of standard agenda items, including:
- unauthorized changes
- authorized changes not handled by the CAB
- RFCs that must be reviewed by the CAB members
- ongoing or closed changes
- assessment of implemented changes

No change should be approved without having an answer to the following question: "what will we do if the change is unsuccessful?" You must always ensure that a **fallback situation (remediation planning)** is available.

Activities, methods and techniques

Overall the change management activities include:

- change planning and control
- change and Release scheduling
- communications
- change decision making and authorization
- ensuring there are remediation plans
- measurement and control
- management reporting
- understanding impact
- continual improvement

The specific activities to manage individual changes are discussed in subsequent sections (see Figure 5.2):

1. create and record RFC
2. review the RFC and change proposal
3. assess and evaluate the change
4. authorize the change
5. plan updates
6. coordinate change implementation
7. review and close change

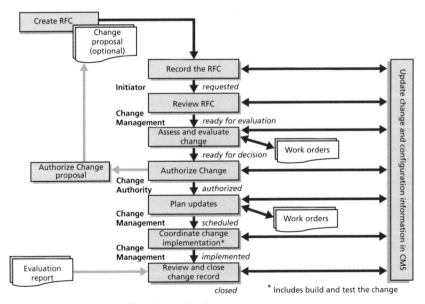

Figure 5.2 Example process flow of a regular change

This section outlines the aspects followed within a "normal" change. The general principles set out apply to all changes and the "normal" change procedure is modified accordingly to deal with standard and emergency changes for example.

1. Create and record

The change is raised by a request from the initiator - the individual or organizational group that requires the change. For example, this may be a business unit that requires additional facilities, or problem management staff instigating an error resolution from many other sources.

All RFCs are registered and it must be possible to identify them via a unique identification number.

The scope and impact of the eventual change determine how much information is required for the change.

2. Review the RFC

After registration, the stakeholders verify whether the RFC is: totally impractical, repeats of earlier RFCs, accepted, rejected or still under consideration, incomplete submissions e.g. inadequate description, without necessary budgetary approval. Such requests are rejected and returned to the initiator with details of the reason for the rejection. The initiator should have a right of appeal against rejection.

3. Assess and evaluate changes

This step starts with **categorizing** the change. The issue of risk must be considered prior to the authorization of any change. The **likelihood** that the risk will occur and its possible **impact** determine the **risk category** of the change. In practice, a risk categorization matrix is generally used for this purpose (Figure 5.3).

After the change has been categorized, it is **evaluated**. Based on the impact, risk assessment, potential benefits and costs of the change, the **change authority** (e.g. the change manager and/or CAB) determine whether the change is supported or not.

The following questions must be answered for all changes. Without this information, the impact assessment cannot be completed, and the balance of risk and benefit to the live service will not be understood. The **seven Rs of change management** represent a good starting point for impact analysis:
1. Who raised the change? (Raised)
2. What is the reason for the change? (Reason)

Change Impact	High impact Low probability Risk category: 2	High impact High probability Risk category: 1
	Low impact Low probability Risk category: 4	Low impact High probability Risk category: 3
	Probability	

Figure 5.3 Example of a risk categorization matrix

3. What is the return required from the change? (Return)
4. What are the change's risks? (Risk)
5. What resources does it require? (Resources)
6. Who are responsible for build, testing and implementation? (Responsible)
7. Which relationships exist between this and other changes? (Relationship)

Determine the change's **priority** to establish the order in which the changes put forward must be considered. Priority is derived from the agreed impact and urgency. **Impact** is based on the beneficial change to the business that will result or on the degree of damage and cost to the business if it fails. **Urgency** indicates how long implementation can be delayed.

Examples of priority codes are:
- **low priority** - a change is desirable but can wait until a suitable opportunity occurs
- **medium priority** - no huge urgency or high impact, but the change must not be delayed until a later time; the Change Advisory Board gives this change average priority when allocating resources
- **high priority** - this change represents a serious failure for a number of users or an annoying failure for a large group of users, or it is related to other urgent issues; the Change Advisory Board gives this change top priority in its next meeting
- **immediate priority** - causing significant loss of revenue or the ability to deliver important public services; immediate action is required

Change planning and scheduling

Change management schedules the changes on the change calendar: the **Schedule of Change** (SC). The SC contains the details for all approved changes and their planning e.g. implementation dates.

Changes can be bundled into a release. In consultation with the relevant IT departments, the CAB may set up fixed times to implement changes - moments where services will be hindered as little as possible by changes. A recovery plan must be prepared in case a change implementation is unsuccessful.

4. Authorize the change

Formal authorization from a change authority is required for every change. This may be a role, person or group of people. The level at which approval is required depends on the change type. An example is shown in Figure 5.4.

Figure 5.4 Example of an authorization model

5. Coordinate change implementation

Authorized RFCs should be passed on to the relevant technical groups for building of the changes. Building and creating a release are issues discussed in the Section on "Release and deployment management".

You should **test** the changes, the remediation and the implementation method for the changes thoroughly. Section "Service validation and testing" discusses testing in detail.

6. Review and close change record
Implemented changes - perhaps with the exception of standard changes - are evaluated after some time. The CAB then determines whether further follow-up is required. The CAB pays attention to the following matters:
• Did the change realize its intended purpose?
• Are all the stakeholders satisfied with the outcome?
• Did any side-effects occur?
• Were the estimated costs and effort exceeded?

If the change is successful, it can be closed. The outcome should be included in the **Post Implementation Review** (**PIR**): the change evaluation. If the change is unsuccessful, change management or the CAB decides what should be done. A new or modified RFC may result.

Interfaces
Examples of change types that **trigger** the change management process:
• strategic changes
• changes to one or more services
• operational changes
• changes for continual improvement (See also CSI in Chapter 13)

The **input** of change management includes:
• policies and strategies for change and release
• RFCs
• Change proposal
• Plans - change, transition, release and deployment test, evaluation, remediation
• Schedule of Change and Projected Service Outages (PSOs)
• assets and CIs
• test results, test report and evaluation report

The **output** of change management includes:
• rejected and approved RFCs
• new or changed services, CIs, assets
• adjusted PSO

- updated Schedule of Change
- change decisions, actions, documents, records and reports

Change management has **interfaces** with the change processes of the business, and with program and project management, and with sourcing and partnering. Interfaces with other service management processes:

- **asset and configuration management** - the information from the configuration management system (CMS) helps to determine the impact of the proposed changes and track the workflow of the changes; it also shows which related CIs (those not included in the RFC) are impacted by the change; Figure 5.5 shows how change and configuration management collaborate
- **problem management** - problem management is one of the parties that most frequently submits RFCs and makes an important contribution to CAB discussions
- **IT service continuity management** - this process has many procedures and plans that are updated by the change management process
- **information security management** - all changes relating to security issues are handled via the change management process
- **capacity and demand management** - badly managed demand results in a great many risks; capacity management plays an important part in the assessment of changes

*Includes build and test where applicable

Figure 5.5 The workflow of change and configuration management

Metrics

KPIs for the change management process include:

- the number of implemented changes that comply with the customer specifications
- the benefits of the change compared to the costs
- the reduction of the number of service interruptions
- the reduction of the number of unauthorized changes
- the reduction of the number of backouts
- change success rate after evaluation compared to the number of approved RFCs
- the reduction of the number of unplanned changes

Examples of metrics for the change management process:

- **Output metrics,** such as:
  - number of disruptions, incidents and problems resulting from changes
  - number of inaccurate change specifications
  - number of incomplete impact analyses
  - service/application repair work resulting from inaccurate change specifications
- **Workload metrics,** such as:
  - frequency of changes
  - number of changes
- **Process metrics,** such as:
  - people's satisfaction with speed, clarity and ease of use
  - number and rate of changes that follow formal change management procedures
  - ratio of planned versus unplanned RFCs
  - ratio of accepted versus rejected RFCs
  - staff utilization
  - costs versus budget

5.3 Service Asset and Configuration Management

Introduction
The **purpose** of Service Asset and Configuration Management (SACM) is to provide a logical model of the IT infrastructure. In this model the IT services are related to the different IT components needed to supply these services.

The **objective** is: to define service and infrastructure components and maintain accurate configuration records. In this context it is important that:
- the integrity of the service assets and Configuration Items (CIs) are protected
- all assets and CIs are located in configuration management system
- the operational and service management processes are supported effectively

Scope
All assets that are used during the Service Lifecycle fall within the scope of asset management. The process offers a complete overview of all assets, and shows who is responsible for the control and maintenance of these assets.

Configuration management ensures that all components (CIs) that form part of the service or product are identified, **baselined** (the configuration) and maintained. It ensures that releases into controlled environments and operational use are on the basis of formal approvals. The process also provides a logical model of all services, assets, the physical infrastructure and the mutual relations.

SACM also relates to non-IT assets and CIs, such as work products used to develop the services and configurations items required to support the service that are not formally classified as assets. The scope of the process also includes assets and CIs of other suppliers ("shared assets"), to the extent that they are relevant to the service.

Value for the business
SACM increases the visibility and performance of the service, release or environment. Among other things this results in:
- better forecasting and planning of changes
- changes and releases to be assessed, planned and successfully delivered
- incidents and problems to be resolved within the service level targets
- better adherence to standards, legal and regulatory obligations (less non-conformances)
- ability to identify the costs for a service

Policies

The first step is to develop and maintain the SACM policies that set the objectives, scope and principles and critical success factors for what is to be achieved by the process. There are significant costs and resource implications to implementing SACM and therefore strategic decisions need to be made about the priorities to be addressed. Many IT service providers focus initially on the basic IT assets (hardware and software) and services that are business critical or covered by legal and regulatory compliance e.g. SOX, software licensing.

Starting points

The policies describe the starting points for the development and control of assets and CIs, for instance:

- the costs of SACM are proportionate to the potential risks to the service if SACM were not implemented
- the need to provide specifications for "corporate governance"
- the need to guarantee the agreements in the SLA and other contracts
- the specifications for available, reliable and cost-effective services
- the specifications for performance criteria
- the transition from reactive maintenance to proactive control
- the requirement to maintain adequate asset and configuration information for stakeholders

Basic concepts

By maintaining relations between CIs a **logical model** of the services, assets and infrastructure (Figure 5.6) is created. This enables other processes to access valuable information:

- impact analysis for proposed changes
- investigations into the cause of incidents and problems
- the planning and design of changes, software upgrades and technological refresh
- the planning of release and deployment packages
- optimization of the use of assets and costs

ITIL defines a **configuration item** as follows:

A **configuration item** is an asset, service component or other item that is (or will be) under the control of configuration management.

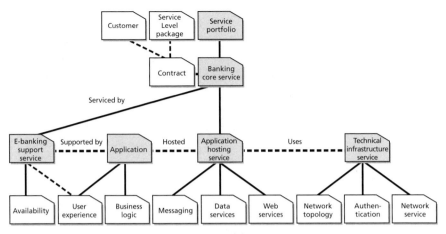

Figure 5.6 An example of a logical configuration model

There are many types of CIs, such as:
- service lifecycle CIs - CIs for the support of the Service Lifecycle activities, such as the business case and release and change plans
- service CIs, such as service capability assets, service resource assets, service model, service package, release package, service acceptance criteria
- organizational CIs, such as the documentation relating to the strategy of the organization
- internal CIs, for instance those associated with individual projects
- external CIs, such as specifications of external customer requirements and agreements
- interface CIs that are required to deliver the end to end service across a Service Provider Interface (SPI)

In order to manage large and complex IT services and infrastructures SACM needs to use a supporting system: a **Configuration Management System (CMS).**

A CMS generally consists of four layers:
- a **presentation layer** with different "views" for the different target groups
- a **knowledge processing layer** for, for instance, producing reports and queries
- an **information integration layer** that collates and structures the data
- a **data layer** with the data and information from different sources such as configuration management databases (**CMDBs**), discovery and inventory tools, project information, etc.

Figure 5.7 shows an example of a CMS.

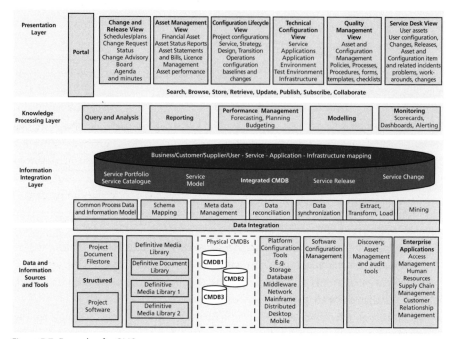

Figure 5.7 Example of a CMS

At data level it may be that the CMS gets its data from different CMDBs that, together, form a **federated CMDB**. In practice, it frequently happens that some elements of a service are outsourced, whereas others are performed in-house. For instance, the network is outsourced to service provider A and the server management to service provider B, whereas the application management is performed in-house. In this case the CMS will need data from three different CMDBs that are controlled (and owned) by three different parties.

Where possible, use automated tools (such as discovery, inventory and audit tools) to populate and maintain the CMDB. This minimizes the opportunity for error and saves costs.

ITIL defines various **libraries**:
- A **secure library** is a collection of software, electronic or document CIs of a known type and status.

- A **secure store** is a secure location where IT assets are stored.
- The **Definitive Media Library (DML)** is a secure store where the definitive, authorized (approved) versions of all media CIs are stored and protected.
- **Definitive spares** are an area set aside for secure storage of definitive hardware spares.

It must be possible for all libraries of physical and electronic media to be uniquely identifiable and to be documented in the CMS.

A **configuration baseline** is a configuration of a service, product or infrastructure that has been formally reviewed and agreed on that thereafter serves as the basis for further activities, and that can be changed only through formal change procedures. Among other uses a baseline is used:
- to mark a milestone in the development of a service (e.g. Service Design baseline)
- to build a service component from a defined set of inputs
- to change or rebuild a specific version at a later stage
- to assemble all relevant components in readiness for a change or release
- as a fall-back in the case of problems with new configurations (after changes)

Baseline configurations are included in the CMS.

A **snapshot** (moment in time) is the most recent status of a CI or environment (for instance as it was inventoried by a discovery tool). A snapshot is stored in the CMS and is kept as a read-only historical record (i.e. it cannot be changed). A snapshot:
- is convenient for problem management to analyze what the situation was at the time incidents occurred
- facilitates system restore to support security scanning software

Activities, methods and techniques
The basic SACM process activities consist of:
1. management and planning
2. configuration identification
3. configuration control
4. status accounting and reporting
5. verification and audit

1. Management and planning
The management team and configuration management decide what level of configuration management is needed and how this level will be achieved. This is documented in a

configuration management plan. Contents of a configuration management plan include:
- context and objective
- scope
- requirements
- applicable policies and standards
- organization for configuration management including roles and responsibilities
- SACM systems and tools
- selection and application of processes and procedures to implement SACM activities including configuration identification, version management, build management, etc.
- reference implementation plan
- relationship management and interface controls e.g. with financial asset management, with projects, with development and customers, etc.
- relationship management and control of service providers and sub-contractors

2. Configuration identification

Configuration identification focuses on determining and maintaining the naming and version numbering of assets and CIs, the mutual relations and the relevant attributes. The most important activities of configuration identification are:
- defining and documenting criteria for the selection of CIs and the components within them
- selecting the CIs on the basis of the defined criteria
- giving all CIs unique numbers for identification purposes
- specifying the attributes of each CI
- indicating when each CI will be placed under configuration management
- identifying the "owner" of each CI

Create a **configuration structure** for each IT service. This structure shows the relations and hierarchy between CIs for a certain service. The configuration structure has a top-down approach. The highest level is the service in question. The lowest CI level is determined by:
- the available information
- the necessary level of control
- the necessary resources required to maintain that CI level

It is only useful to include a certain CI if it supports the other service management processes.

Document **naming conventions** and apply them in the identification of CIs, documents and changes, but also, for instance, in basic configurations, releases and compilations.

Each CI must be uniquely identifiable by means of a version number, as there may be several versions of the same CI; for example different versions of software. When planning naming conventions allow for future growth. The names must also be short but meaningful, and correspond with the existing conventions as much as possible.

Provide all physical CIs, such as hardware, with **labels**, so that they are easy to identify. The labels must be easy to read and accessible, so that a user can pass the information on the label on to the service desk. Labels with a barcode are very efficient for physical audits of the CIs. During such audits it is checked whether the CIs in the organization correspond with those within the CMS.

With the aid of **attributes** information is stored that is relevant for the CI in question. When structuring the CMDB the following attributes, among others, can be used:
- CI number / label or barcode number - unique identifier
- CI type
- name / description
- version
- location
- supply date
- licence details e.g. expiry date
- owner
- status
- supplier / source
- related documents
- related software
- historical data e.g. audit trail
- relationship type
- applicable SLA
- purchase date
- acceptance date
- current status
- planned status
- purchase value
- residual value after depreciation
- comments

The characteristics of a CI are often recorded in **configuration documentation**. Table 5.1 is a RACI table (*Responsible, Accountable, Consulted, Informed*) that shows different documentation types of service CIs and indicates who takes responsibility for the documents in the different phases of the Service Lifecycle.

Service Life-cycle State	Examples of Service Lifecycle Assets and CIs impacted	Service Strategy	Service Design	Service Transition	Service operations	CSI
Service Strategy	Portfolios – Service contract, customer	A	C	C	R	C
	Service Strategy requirements					
	Service Lifecycle Model					
Service Design	Service Package (including SLA)	I	A	C	R	C
	Service Design Package e.g.					
	Service Model, Contract					
	Supplier's service management plan. Process interface definition.					
	Customer Engagement plan					
	Release Policy					
	Release package definition					
Service Transition	Service Transition model	I	C	A	R	C
	Test plan					
	Controlled environments					
	Build/installation plan					
	Build specification					
	Release plan					
	Deployment plan					
	CMS					
	SKMS					
	Release package					
	Release baseline					
	Release documentation					
	Test report					
Service Operations	Service Operations model	I	C	C	A/R	R
	Service Support model					
	Service Desk					
	User assets					
	User documentation					
	Operations documentation					
	Support documentation					
Continual Service Improvement	CSI model	A/C	A/C	A/C	R	A
	Service improvement plan					
	Service reporting process					

Table 5.1 RACI table for configuration documentation in the lifecycle

Relationships describe how CIs work together to provide a service. The CMDB maintains these relations to demonstrate the interdependencies between CIs, for instance:

- a CI **is part of** another CI - a software module is part of an application (parent-child relation)
- a CI **is connected to** - a PC that is connected to the LAN
- a CI **uses** another CI - a business service uses a server
- a CI **is installed** on another CI - MS Word is installed on a PC

Relationships are also the mechanism for associating RFCs, incidents, problems, known errors and releases to CIs. Relations can be 1-to-1, 1-to-n and n-to-1.

CIs are classed by means of a **classification**, for instance: service, hardware, software documentation, personnel.

A **release unit** is the portion of the service or infrastructure, that is normally released together, in accordance with an organizations release policy. Releases are documented in the CMS for the support of the release and deployment process.

Releases can be classified into the following **release categories**:

- major releases - important deployment of new hardware and software with, in most cases, a considerable expansion of the functionality (V1.0, 2.0, etc.)
- minor releases - these usually contain a number of smaller improvements; some of these improvements were previously implemented as quick fixes but are now included integrally within a release (V1.1, V1.2, etc.)
- emergency releases - usually implemented as a temporary solution for a problem or known error (V1.1.1, V1.1.2, etc.)

3. Configuration control

Configuration control ensures that the CIs are adequately managed. No CIs can be added, modified, replaced or removed without following the agreed procedure. Establish guidelines and procedures for, among others:

- license management
- change management
- version management
- access control
- build control
- promotion
- deployment

- installation
- baseline configurations integrity management

4. Status accounting and reporting

The lifecycle of a component is classified into different stages and the stages that different types of CI go through must be properly documented. For instance, a release goes through the following stages: registered, accepted, installed, withdrawn.

Status reports give an insight into the current and historical data of each CI and the status changes that have occurred.

Different types of **service asset and configuration reports** are needed for configuration management. The reports may relate to individuals CIs, but also to a complete service. Such reports may consist of:
- a list of CIs and their baseline
- details on the current status and change history
- a list of unauthorized CIs detected
- reports on the unauthorized use of hardware and software

5. Verification and audit

SACM conducts audits to ensure that:
- there are no discrepancies between the documented baselines and the actual business environment to which they refer
- CIs physically exist in the organization or DML and spares stores, the functional and operational characteristics of CIs can be verified and checks can be made that records in the CM match the physical infrastructure
- release and configuration documentation is present before the release is rolled out

Document all exceptions that result from the audits and report them. Corrective actions (CIs that need to be added, changed or deleted) are handled via the change management process.

Audits are conducted at the following times:
- shortly after changes to the CMS
- before and after changes to IT services or infrastructure
- at random and planned intervals
- before a release to ensure the environment is as expected
- in response to the detection of unauthorized CIs
- following recovery from disasters

Audit tools can perform checks at regular intervals, for instance weekly. For example a desktop audit tool that compares the configuration of an individual's desktop against the "master" configuration that was installed.

Information management
Run backups of the CMS on a regular basis and save these in a secure place in a different location in case of any emergencies such as fire.

The CMS maintains information about backups of CIs, historical information on CIs, different versions of CIs and removed versions.

Interfaces
Updates to assets and CIs are **triggered** by RFCs, service requests and new assets and CIs.

SACM supports and has **interfaces** with all other service management processes. The most notable of these are:
- **change management** - for impact analyses
- **financial management** - for insight into costs, depreciations, maintenance and repairs
- **IT service continuity management** - to make the organization aware of the assets the business depends on, and for the control of key spares and software
- **incident and problem management** - for the diagnosis of problems and incidents
- **availability management** - for the detection of "points or failure"

SACM also has many **interactions** with release and deployment management. These processes benefit greatly from an integrated approach with SACM.

Metrics
The following **measures** are used to evaluate the performance of the SACM process:
- increased quality and accuracy of information about assets and CIs
- fewer errors as a result of outdated information
- shorter audits because the information is more accessible
- shorter diagnosis and resolution times for problems and incidents
- fewer discrepancies between the actual situation and that in the CMS

Implementation

Among others, the **challenges** in the SACM process are:
- convincing staff that they cannot circumvent the SACM process
- finding and justifying financial resources for SACM
- collecting too much data simply because it is available
- lack of management acceptance and support

Critical success factors of the SACM process are:
- determining the right level of detail and depth
- implementing a top-down approach for the configuration structure
- achieving the right level of accuracy
- using technology to automate the CMS and to enforce SACM guidelines

The following **risks** are acknowledged:
- too much technical focus as opposed to operational and service focus
- the CMS becomes outdated because, for instance, unauthorized personnel move hardware assets

5.4   Release and Deployment Management

Introduction
ITIL defines release and deployment management as follows:

> ***Release and deployment management*** *aims to build, test and deliver the capability to provide the services specified by service design and that will accomplish the stakeholders' requirements and deliver the intended objectives.*

The **goal** of release and deployment management is the deployment of releases into production, and the establishment of effective use of the service in order to deliver value to the customer and to be able to handover to service operations.

The **objective** of release and deployment management is to ensure that:
- release and deployment plans are in place
- release packages (compilation) are deployed successfully
- knowledge transfer to the customers takes place
- there is minimum disruption to the services

Scope
The processes, systems and functions for packaging, building, testing and deployment of a release into production and establishment of the service specified in the service design package before final handover to service operations.

Value for the business
Effective release and deployment management contributes to the business because:
- changes are realized faster, cheaper and with fewer risks, and the operational objectives are supported better
- the implementation approach is more consistent and the traceability requirements (e.g. audits, legislation etc.) are complied with more closely

Basic concepts

> *A **release** is a set of new or changed CIs that are tested and will be implemented into production together.*

A **release unit** is the portion of the service or infrastructure that is included in the release, in accordance with the organization's release guidelines.

It is important to determine the correct level of the release. For a business critical application it may make sense to include the complete application in the release unit, but for a website it may only have to be the HTML page that is changed.

In the **release design** different considerations apply in respect of the way in which the release is deployed. The most frequently occurring options for the rollout of releases are:

- **Big bang versus phased** - A big bang release deploys the new or changed service for all the users at the same time. A phased deployment deploys the release for part of the user base at a time.
- **Push and pull** - With a push approach the service component is deployment from the "center" to the target locations. With a pull approach the new release is made available to the users from a central location from which they download to their location at a time they choose.
- **Automated or manual** - Releases can, to a large extent, be automated; e.g. the use of installation software.

The release and deployment teams must have a good understanding of the relevant IT architecture involved in a release and deployment process. This understanding is essential to determine the sequence in which the activities are implemented and for mapping out all the interdependencies.

A **release package** is a single release unit or a structured set of release units. In the case of a new or a changed service all the elements of which the service consists - the infrastructure, hardware, software, applications, documentation, knowledge, etc. - must be taken into account. See Figure 5.8. For different types of packages, see 5.3 (SACM).

Activities, methods and techniques

The basic process activities of release and deployment management consist of:

1. planning
2. preparation for building, testing and deployment
3. building and testing
4. service testing and pilots
5. planning and preparing the deployment
6. transfer, deployment, and retirement
7. verify deployment

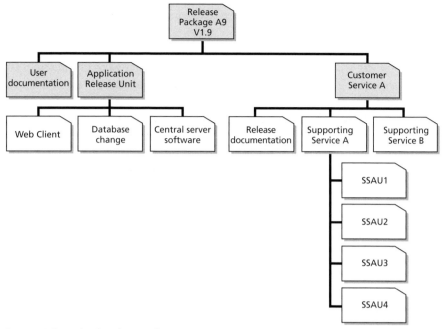

Figure 5.8 Example of a release package

8. Early Life Support (ELS)
9. review and close

1. Planning
Prior to a deployment into production different plans are formulated. The type and number depends on the size and complexity of the environment and the changed or new service. Release and deployment plans form part of the overall Service Transition plan. Change management will approve or reject the plans. The plans will include the following:
- scope, content, risks, responsibilities and stakeholders in the release
- team responsible for the release
- approach for collaboration with all stakeholders

The following (sub) plans are relevant for release and deployment:
- **Pass/fail criteria** - Service Transition is responsible for the planning the pass/fail situations for every phase of the release and deployment.
- **Building and test plans** - Building and test plans are needed that describe the approach to the building, testing and maintenance of the pre-production environment; different

environments are needed for each test type: for unit testing, service release testing and integration testing.

The V model is a convenient tool for mapping out the different configuration levels at which building and testing must take place. The left side of the V in this example starts with service specifications and ends with the detailed Service Design. The right side of the V reflects the test activities, by means of which the specifications on the left-hand side must be validated. In the middle we find the test and validation criteria (Figure 5.9).

- **Planning of pilots** - To test the new or changed service with part of the users first, a pilot can be planned; do not forget to include in the plans how the feedback from the users is to be collected and processed, and devise a rollout scenario.
- **Planning of release package (compilation) and build** - Formulate plans and procedures for:
  - pass/fail criteria
  - the management of changes and the communication with stakeholders
  - training of staff, knowledge transfer and readiness assessment of end users
  - the use of (service management) resources
  - the transfer of systems and users to the new service
- **Deployment planning** - With regard to deployment include the following considerations in the plan:
  - What is being deployed?
  - Who are the users?
  - What is the local situation?
  - Where are the users?
  - Who else needs to be notified?
  - Why is there a deployment?
  - What are the Critical Success Factors?
- **Logistical planning and delivery planning** - Once the deployment approach has been decided, logistical and delivery plans will be formulated with attention for the following points:
  - when and how will the service components be delivered
  - what should be done if there are delays
  - managing customs and other implications of international distributions
- **Financial and commercial planning** - Financial and commercial aspects must be checked before the deployment takes place.

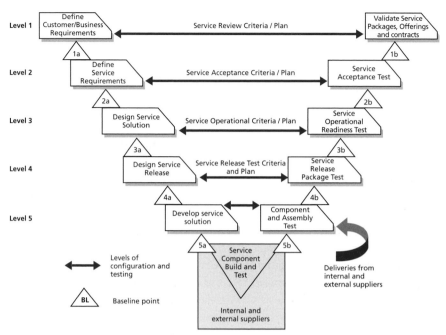

Figure 5.9 The service V model that reflects configuration and test levels

2. Preparation for building (compilation), testing and deployment

Before approval can be given for the building and test phase, the service and release design is compared against the specifications of the new or changed service (validation). This comparison may highlight risks or issues relating to the service, the assets and CIs. These issues or risks are then prioritized and actions are undertaken to resolve them in good time. The service evaluation report documents the results of the validation.

3. Building and testing

The build and test phase of the release consists of the following activities:

- **Management of general (common) infrastructure and services** - Carefully manage the common services and infrastructure, as they may be of significant importance to the building and testing.
- **Use of release and building documentation** - The available documentation (procedures, templates, manuals) must be used throughout; this documentation supports the release team in acquiring and purchasing assets, CIs, services and products for the construction of an integrated release package; in this context also consider proof of licenses (it must be possible to produce the required licenses) of the various components.

- **Acquisition, purchasing and testing of CIs and components for the release** - CIs and components are acquired from projects, suppliers and partners; the purchasing activities include:
  - the recording or updating of the CIs in the CMS
  - ensuring that the licenses can be produced when necessary; also check the CIs and components for quality, legality and the requirements with respect to labeling and naming
- **Compilation of the release (release packaging)** - The key activities for building and compiling a release package are:
  - assembling and integrating the components
  - preparing the compilation and release documentation
  - installing and checking the release package
  - creating a baseline of the composition of the package
  - formulating a service message (that the release package is ready for use)
- **Structuring and controlling the test environments** - The test environments must be stable and able to be controlled.

4. Service testing and pilots

Test management is responsible for the coordination of the test activities and the planning and control of the implementation. Section 5.5 "Service validation and testing" comprehensively describes test management.

In this paragraph we limit ourselves to the tests that are conducted during the release and deployment process:

- **Service release test** - The service release test checks whether the service components work well together (integration), and that the release can be compiled, installed and tested in the target environment.
- **Service Operation "readiness testing"** - This test ensures that the service and the underlying applications and technical infrastructure can be transferred to the live environment in a controlled manner.
- **Pilots** - A pilot is intended to test whether there are elements of the service that do not meet specifications, or may pose a risk to the business.

5. Planning and preparing for deployment

These activities prepare the deployment group for deployment. The following need to be addressed:

- Are they ready for the implementation of the release package?
- Have they prepared the activity plan?
- Have the potential risks been mapped out?

- Is everyone sufficiently trained?
- Have there been any last-minute changes in the specifications?

In addition, the other aspects the team will be faced with are also assessed, such as financial aspects, the extent to which the organization is prepared, the infrastructure and other facilities and the available service management resources.

When planning a specific deployment, plans include: risk limitation, transfers, upgrades, logistical matters, knowledge transfer and communication. Finally, these plans have to be evaluated and an RFC must be created that is submitted to change management for approval. After this the service is ready for deployment.

6. Transfer, deployment, and retirement
The following activities are important during the deployment:
- **The transfer of financial assets** - This may be, for instance, the transfer of support and maintenance costs, license fees and contingency reserves (disaster recovery) to a third party.
- **Transfer and transition of business and organization** - When a service or service unit is transferred the organization itself will also have to be adapted; consider, for instance, new tasks, authorities and responsibilities.
- **Publication of documentation** - Distribute all documentation (guidelines, processes, procedures, manuals) that the users will need to take the new service into use.
- **Transfer of "service management capability"** - Transfer new or changed process information, systems and tools to the team that is responsible for the service management activities.
- **Transfer of the service** - Activities that are relevant in this process include:
  - analysis of service performance, issues and risks
  - configuration audits of service assets
  - updating of service catalogue
  - distribution of service notification
- **Deployment of the service** - All activities needed to distribute and install the service.
- **Cancellation of services** - Cancel redundant services.
- **Removal of redundant assets** - Remove assets that are redundant as a result of the new or changed service.

7. Verify deployment
When all the deployment activities have been completed it is important to verify that all the users, service operations, other staff and stakeholders are able to use the service

as intended. This is also a good time to collect feedback on the deployment. Use this information for the improvement of future deployments.

8. Early life support

Early Life Support (ELS) is intended to offer extra support after the deployment of a new or changed service. ELS provides the means to resolve operational and support problems as quickly as possible, which means that users do not have to be confronted with service interruptions. These may be "teething problems" or improvements that can help to stabilize the service.

The deployment team also updates the documentation during the ELS phase and updates the knowledge bank with additional diagnostic information, known errors, workarounds and FAQs. Service Transition will monitor the performance of the new or changed service during the ELS phase until all the exit criteria have been met, including:
- all users are able to use the service effectively and efficiently
- service and process owners are able to manage the service
- agreed service and performance levels are achieved

9. Review and close

In the review of a deployment, check whether:
- the knowledge transfer and training were adequate
- all user experiences have been documented
- all fixes and changes are complete and all problems, known errors and workarounds have been documented
- the quality criteria have been complied with
- the service is ready for transition from ELS into production

Also check whether there are issues that have to be passed on to CSI. The deployment is completed when the support is transferred to Operations. Finally, change management will conduct a Post Implementation Review (PIR).

To finalize the Service Transition as a whole a formal evaluation must be performed that is tailored to with the scale and scope of the change.

Information management

As CIs are deployed successfully the CMS is updated with information such as:
- new or changed CIs
- relationships between requirements and test cases
- installation and build plans

- logistics and delivery plans
- validation and test plans
- new or change locations and users
- status updates
- changes of ownership (of assets and CIs)
- licenses

Also, documented information for the service knowledge management system, such as information about the deployment, training and known errors, may be necessary.

Interfaces
The release process is triggered by an approved RFC.

Inputs for the release and deployment process are:
- approved RFC, service package, SLP, SDP, SAC, continuity plans
- release policies, design and model, construction model and plan
- technology, purchasing, service management and operation standards and plans
- exit and entry criteria for each phase of the release and deployment

Outputs from the release and deployment process are:
- release and deployment plans, completed RFC, service notifications, an updated service catalogue and service model
- new or changed service management documentation and service reports
- new tested service capability and environment
- SLA, OLAs and contracts
- Service Transition report and service capacity plan
- complete and accurate CI list with an audit trail for the CIs in the release package and also the new of changed service and infrastructure configurations

Metrics
Customer-related KPIs include:
- improvement of service performance
- reduction of the number of incidents
- improvement of customer and user satisfaction

Supplier-related KPIs include:
- lower costs for the diagnosis of incidents and problems
- reduction in the number of discrepancies in configuration audits compared with the real world

Implementation

Challenges in the release and deployment process include:

- the development of standard performance measurements and methods across projects and suppliers
- dependence on projects and suppliers
- understanding all the risks that may affect the Service Transition
- understanding the perspectives and starting points of the different stakeholders

Critical success factors in the release and deployment process include:

- new (or changed) service runs in the target environment and is tested against the Service Design
- new (or changed) service has proven itself in a pilot
- test models are re-usable for regression tests in future releases

Risks in the release and deployment process are:

- lack of clarity in the expectations and objectives of different stakeholders, ill-defined roles, tasks and responsibilities
- incompetent management, insufficient financial resources, lack of control, poor change management
- poor relationships with partners and service providers, insufficient support (commitment) from stakeholders
- risks relating to the technical infrastructure and applications

5.5   Service Validation and Testing

Introduction
Testing of services is an important contribution to the quality of IT service provision. Testing ensures that new (or changed) services are **fit for purpose** and **fit for use**.

Fit for purpose means that the service does what the client expects of it, so that the service supports the business. "Fit for use" addresses such aspects as availability, continuity, capacity and security of the service.

Insufficient attention to testing may result in: increase of incidents, issues and errors, extra service desk phone calls with questions regarding the functioning of the service, higher costs and a service that is improperly used.

The **goal** of service validation and testing is to provide a service that adds value to the customers and their business.

The **objective** of service validation and testing is to make sure that:
- the release delivers the expected outcomes and value for the customers within projected costs, capacity and constraints
- services are fit for purpose and fit for use
- specifications (requirements) by customer and other stakeholders are met

Scope
Service validation and testing is applied during the entire Service Lifecycle, and is aimed at testing the quality of service (units), and intended to verify whether the service provider has sufficient capacity and resources in order to provide a service or service release successfully.

Testing is also particularly supportive of the release and deployment processes. In addition, the evaluation process will be using test results.

Value for the business
Service interruptions may be damaging to business operations of service provider and clients who are recipients of the services. They may result in damage to reputation, financial loss and even (fatal) accidents. For example, the role of IT in hospitals, the automotive or aerospace industries can mean injury or death if service delivery fails.

Basic concepts

The **service model** describes the structure and dynamics of a service provided by Service Operation. The structure consists of core and supporting services and service assets needed. When a new (or changed) service is designed, developed and built, these service assets are tested in relation to design specifications and requirements. Activities, flow of resources, coordination, and interactions describe the dynamics (see Figure 5.10).

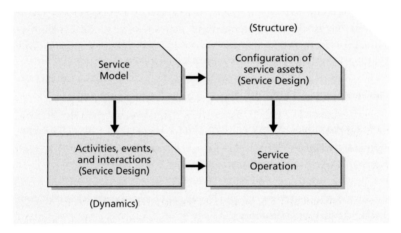

Figure 5.10 Service models describe the structure and dynamics of a service

Policies for service validation and testing are:
* service quality policies
* risk policies
* reusability policies
* Service Transition policies
* release policies
* mandatory integral testing
* involving all stakeholders in testing
* change management policies

The **test strategy** defines the overall testing approach and the allocation of required resources. This strategy might be applicable to the entire organization, a collection of services or an individual service. All test strategies are developed in collaboration with the stakeholders. Attention is paid to objectives, scope, standards, test processes, test metrics, test approach, requirements of man and means and "deliverables".

A **test model** consists of a test plan, what is to be tested and test scripts which indicate the method by which each element must be tested. In order to ensure that the process can be repeated, test models must be structured in such a way that:
- the specification or design criteria being tested can be traced
- test activities, evaluation and reports can be audited
- test elements can be maintained and changed

Whether or not testing is effective will be determined, in part, by the degree to which the service meets requirements. These requirements, in turn, are based on the perspectives of those who use, provide, deploy or manage the service. The Service Design package therefore defines entry and exit criteria for all **test perspectives**.

By using **test models**, such as a **V model** (Figure 5.9) "validating and testing" becomes a part of the Service Lifecycle early in the process. The V model provides a useful framework for organizing the levels at which CIs must be managed. It also helps to determine which test activity should take place at which level. Tests can take place both within and between various levels.

There are very many different **test techniques** and **test approaches**. The technique and approach depends on the service type, risk profile, test goal and test level. Examples include: document review, modeling, simulation, scenario testing, role play and laboratory testing, live pilot.

Design considerations that are important for testing relate to finances (is the budget big enough?), documentation (is everything available, and in the correct format?), composition (build), testability (think of resources, time and facilities), traceability (traceable to specifications), when and where testing is to take place, and remediation (is there a backup plan?).

Also remember to take management and maintenance of test data into account in the design. This concerns the separation of test and live data, regulations with respect to data security, backing up of test data, and so on.

In addition to all kinds of functional and non-functional **test types**, role playing is also possible based on perspective (target group):
- **service requirements testing** "fit for purpose" (service provider, users and client) - does the service meet the specifications determined?
- **service level testing** (service level managers, operation managers and clients) - this concerns testing whether the new service meets the service levels determined

- **service assurance testing** "fit for use" (customer) - to verify availability, capacity, continuity and security
- **usability testing** (end users and maintainers) - to verify user-friendliness and usability for groups such as visually impaired users
- **contract and regulation testing** (service providers) - this could be for service providers who must (contractually) comply with ISO/IEC 20000 and industries that must comply with very specific regulations such as the (UK) Ministry of Defence and the pharmaceutical industry
- **service management testing** (service provider) - ISO/IEC 20000 could be used for this; ISO/IEC 20000 indicates the minimum requirements that processes must meet
- **operational testing** (system, services) - these could be stress tests, security and recoverability
- **regression testing** - being able to repeat earlier (successful) tests in order to compare new results with the previous ones

Activities, methods and techniques

Figure 5.11 schematically displays the testing process. The activities are not necessarily performed in this order; they might also take place parallel to each other. The following activities can be distinguished:

1. validation and test management
2. planning and design
3. verification test plan and design
4. prepare test environment
5. testing
6. evaluate exit criteria and report
7. clean up and closure

1. Validation and test management

Test management consists of planning and managing (control), and reporting on the activities taking place during all test phases of the Service Transition. This includes the following activities:

- planning of resources, and what is being tested at what time
- managing incidents, problems, errors, deviations, issues, risks (including during the discovery in the Transition phase)
- collecting test metrics; analyze, report and manage

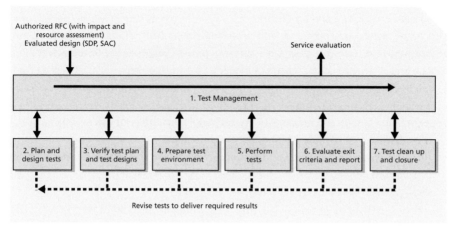

Figure 5.11 Schematic display of the test process

2. Planning and design
Test planning and design activities take place early in the Service Lifecycle and relate to the following:
- resources such as hardware, network, number of staff members, capacity, ability and finances
- business/customer resources required
- supporting services
- schedule of milestones and delivery and acceptance

3. Verification of Test Plan and Design
Test plans and designs are verified to make sure that everything (including scripts) is complete, and that test models sufficiently take into account the risk profile of the service in question and all possible interfaces.

4. Preparation test environment
Prepare the test environment and make a baseline configuration of the test environment.

5. Testing
The tests are executed using manual or automated testing techniques and procedures. Testers register all results. If a test fails, the reason is documented. Proceed with the test as closely as possible according to test plans and scripts. Document the cause of the failure.

6. Evaluate exit criteria and report

The actual results are compared with projected results (exit criteria). Test results can be interpreted in terms of "pass/fail" (approval or not), any risks the tested object may contain for service provider or client, or in terms of costs required to reach the projected goal.

Collect the test results and recapitulate for the report. Examples of exit criteria are:
- the tested service complies with quality requirements
- the service and supporting IT infrastructure will enable the end user to perform all functions as defined
- configuration baselines are captured into the CMS

7. Clean up and closure

Make sure that the test environment is cleaned up. Review the test approach and identify improvements.

Information management

Testing benefits greatly by reuse, and for this reason it is advisable to create a library of relevant tests and ensure that it is up-to-date. Also record the way in which these tests should be executed and implemented.

No matter how well a test is designed, without good **test data**, the test is useless. Therefore, take the upkeep of test data seriously. For this purpose, it is important that:
- test data is separated from live data
- data protection regulations are taken into account
- backup and recovery procedures are in place

Interfaces

Testing is **triggered** by the planned test activity in a release plan, test plan or plan for quality assurance.

Inputs to the test and validation processes are:
- the service package and Service Level Package (SLP)
- interface definitions by the service provider
- Service Design package
- release and deployment plans
- acceptance criteria and RFCs

Outputs of the test and validation process are:
- configuration baselines of the test environment
- testing carried out
- results from the tests
- analysis of results
- test incidents, problems, and error records
- improvement ideas (for CSI)
- updated data
- information and knowledge for the knowledge management system

Tests support all release and deployment steps in the Service Transition process. In addition, testing is **related** to Service Design, CSI, Service Operation and Service Strategy.

Metrics

The effectiveness of testing from a **client perspective** (external) can be measured by:
- reduction in the impact of incidents and errors in production that are attributable to a newly transitioned service
- more effective use of resources and involvement from the customer (e.g. user acceptance tests)
- a better understanding by all stakeholders of the roles and responsibilities that relate to the new or changed service

Service provider related (internal):
The test process must be executed as effectively and efficiently as possible. Potential measures to achieve this are:
- decreased effort and costs in setting up the test environment
- decrease in effort required to discover errors and decrease in the number of "repeated errors"
- reuse of test data
- decrease in the percentage of incidents related to errors discovered during testing
- number of known errors documented during prior test phases

Implementation

The greatest **challenge** still lies in the fact that testing is not taken seriously enough by many organizations. As a result, there is often a lack of funding.

Critical success factors are:
- issues are identified in an early stage of the lifecycle
- quality is built into every phase of the lifecycle, for example by using the V model
- reusable test models are designed, and testing provides the proof that all configurations have been built and implemented according to client requirements

Risks are:
- unclear expectations and objectives, lack of understanding that testing is a critical process in relation to quality of service provision
- lack of resources

5.6 Evaluation

Introduction
ITIL defines the evaluation process as:

> **Evaluation** is a generic process that considers whether the performance of something is acceptable, value for money etc. - and whether it will be proceeded with, accepted into use, paid for etc.

The **objective** of the ITIL evaluation process is to determine the performance of a service change. That performance is assessed on the basis of the predicted (intended) performance.

Scope
In this section, the scope is limited to the evaluation of new or changed services.

Value for the business
Evaluation delivers an important piece of input for CSI and the future improvement of service development and change management.

Policies, starting points and basic concepts
The following **policies** apply:
- Service designs or service changes are evaluated before the being transitioned
- all deviations between predicted and actual performance are managed by the customer (agent), e.g. acceptance yes/no
- the customer is involved in evaluation

The following **starting points** are important in the execution of the process:
- the unintended effects of a change (and its consequences) must be identified
- a service change is evaluated fairly, consistently, openly and objectively

Activities, methods and techniques
The evaluation process consists of the following activities:
1. planning the evaluation
2. evaluating the predicted performance
3. evaluating the actual performance

Figure 5.12 shows the evaluation process including input and output.

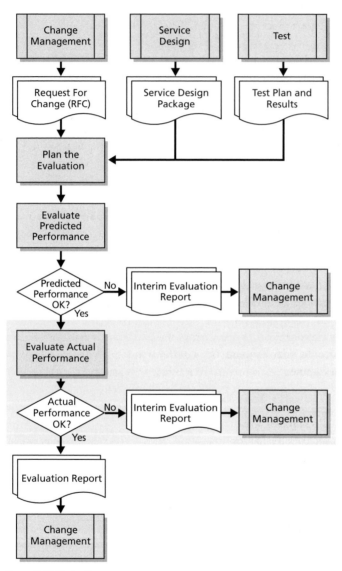

Figure 5.12 Evaluation process

1. Planning the evaluation

When planning an evaluation, the intended and unintended effects of a change are analyzed. The intended effects must meet with the acceptance criteria; the unintended effects are often invisible for a long time and are difficult to predict.

2. Evaluating the predicted performance

Perform a risk assessment based on the customer's requirements (including the acceptance criteria), the predicted performance and the performance model. Send an interim assessment report to change management if the evaluation shows that the predicted performance represents an unacceptable risk to the change or deviates from the acceptance criteria. Cease the evaluation activities while awaiting a decision from change management.

3. Evaluating the actual performance

After implementation of the service change, service operation reports on the actual performance of the service. Perform a second risk assessment, again based on the customer's requirements (including the acceptance criteria), the predicted performance and the performance model. Send a new interim assessment report to change management if the evaluation shows that the actual performance represents an unacceptable risk and cease the evaluation activities while awaiting a decision from change management.

Send an evaluation report to change management if the evaluation is approved. Such a report contains a risk profile, a deviations report, a qualification and validation statement (if necessary), and a recommendation (to accept or refuse the change).

Interfaces

Triggers for the evaluation process are:
- an evaluation request from the Service Transition manager or change management
- an evaluation activity in the project plan

Input for the evaluation process:
- the Service Design Package (SDP)
- Service Acceptance Criteria (SACs)
- test reports
- results

The evaluation report represents the **output**.

Metrics

Customer-related KPIs for evaluation are: differences in service performance (minimal and reducing) and the number of incidents (low and reducing).

Internal KPIs for evaluation are: the number of failed designs (zero) and evaluation time (low and reducing).

Implementation

Challenges include:

- delays in the evaluation schedule due to overdue delivery dates of projects and suppliers
- the development of standard performance measurement methods and creating a "risk management culture"
- considering risks from the various perspectives and building insight into the impact of risks on Service Transition

5.7 Knowledge Management

Introduction
The **goal** of knowledge management is to improve the quality of the (management's) decision-making process by ensuring that reliable and secure information is available during the Service Lifecycle.

The **objectives** of knowledge management are, among others:
- to support the service provider in order to improve the efficiency and quality of the services
- to ensure that the service provider's staff have adequate information available

Scope
Knowledge management is used throughout the entire lifecycle. In ITIL version 3 the book on Service Transition explains the basic principles of the process.

Value for the business
Knowledge management is particularly relevant during Service Transition, since relevant and appropriate knowledge is one of the key service elements being transitioned. Specific examples of the application of knowledge management during Service Transition are:
- training and knowledge transfer, intellectual property, compliance information and standards
- the documentation of errors, workarounds and test information

Basic concepts
Knowledge management is often visualized using the **DIKW** structure: Data-Information-Knowledge-Wisdom, see Figure 5.13.

The basis of the **Service Knowledge Management System (SKMS)** is formed by a considerable amount of data in a central database or configuration management system (CMS) and the CMDB: the CMDB feeds the CMS and the CMS provides input for the SKMS and so supports the decision-making process. However, the scope of the SKMS is broader: information is also stored that relates to matters such as:
- the experience and skills of staff
- information about peripheral matters such as the behavior of users and the performance of the organization
- requirements and expectations of service providers and partners

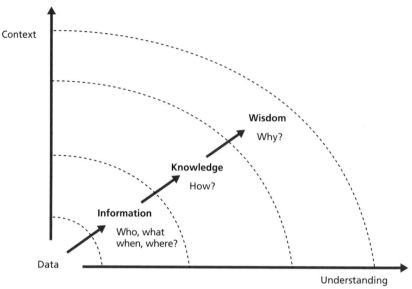

Figure 5.13 DIKW model

Activities, methods and techniques
Knowledge management consists of the following activities, methods and techniques:
1. knowledge management strategy
2. knowledge transfer
3. data and information management
4. the use of the SKMS

1. Knowledge management strategy
An organization needs an overall knowledge management strategy. If such a strategy is already in place, the service management knowledge strategy can link into it. Whether there is an existing strategy or not, the strategy must in any case cover the following elements:
- policies, procedures and methods for knowledge management
- the governance model, forthcoming organizational changes, the definition of roles and responsibilities and the financing
- the required technology and other resources
- performance measures
- establishing roles and responsibilities and ongoing funding

The knowledge management strategy also focuses specifically on documenting relevant knowledge, and on the data and information that support this knowledge.

2. Knowledge transfer

The transfer of knowledge is a challenging task, requiring, in the first place, an analysis to determine what the knowledge gap is between the department or person in possession of the knowledge and those in need of the knowledge. Based on the outcome of this analysis, a communication (improvement) plan is formulated to facilitate the knowledge transfer.

There are a number of knowledge transfer techniques, such as:
- **learning styles** - everyone has a different style of learning; the method must therefore be tailored to the target group in question
- **knowledge visualization** - this technique uses visual aids such as photos, diagrams, pictures and "storyboards" for knowledge transfer
- **driving behavior** - consider, for instance, service desk scripts and compulsory fields in software applications
- **seminars, "webinars", advertisements** - it is very effective to organize a special event for the launch of a new service
- **newsletter, newspaper** - regular communication channels such as newsletters or "e-alerts" lend themselves very well to the transfer of knowledge in small steps (incremental instead of "Big Bang")

3. Information management

Data and information management consists of the following activities:
- **establishing data and information requirements** - data and information are often collected without a clear idea of how the information will be used; this can be very expensive so it pays to determine the requirements first
- **definition of information architecture** - to effectively use data, an architecture needs to be created that corresponds with the requirements and the organization; an example of such an architecture can be seen in Figure 5.14
- **establishing data and information management procedures** - once the requirements and architecture are known the procedures for the control and support of the knowledge management can be formulated
- **evaluation and improvement** - as in all processes, evaluation is needed for the purpose of continual improvement

4. Use of the SKMS

Supplying services to customers in different time zones and regions and with different operating hours imposes strenuous requirements on the sharing of knowledge. For this reason the service provider must develop and maintain an SKMS system that is available to all stakeholders and suits all information requirements. An example of such a system can be seen in Figure 5.14.

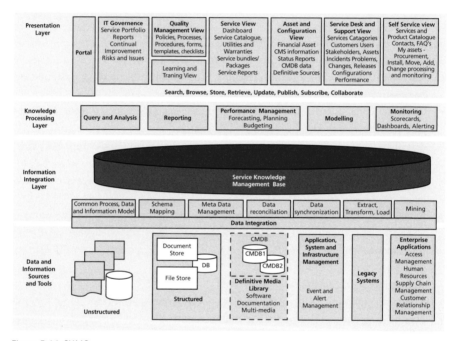

Figure 5.14 SKMS

In addition to material for training and knowledge gathering it is useful to:
- incorporate (IT and business) terminology lists and their translation into the system
- document the operational processes and where they interface with IT
- include SLAs and other contracts that can change as a result of a Service Transition
- include known errors, workarounds and process diagrams

Interfaces

Errors discovered by the **service transition staff** are documented and analyzed. Service Transition makes information accessible to Service Operation regarding the consequences of these errors and any workarounds.

Service Transition staff collect information and data that is returned to Service Design via CSI, and feed back information to Service Design if a change in approach is needed.

Operations staff, like the incident management staff and first and second line staff, are the central "collection point" for information about the day-to-day routine of the managed services. It is essential that this information and knowledge is documented and transferred. Staff working in problem management are important users of this knowledge.

Metrics

Typical **indicators** for the contribution of the IT service provider are:

- successful implementation of new and changed services without few knowledge-related errors
- increased knowledge among target group
- higher number of answered questions
- reduced dependence on personnel for knowledge
- faster identification/location of diagnostic information about incidents and problems

The value of knowledge management to the organization is also determined, however difficult this may be.

Indicators relevant for the customer:

- shorter "early life support"
- shorter problem-solving times
- improved user experience
- fewer unnecessary error reports due to more targeted knowledge transfer

Metrics relevant for the service provider:

- the use of the knowledge base, extent of re-use of documentation
- errors reported by personnel or through an audit
- involvement of personnel in discussion and question/answer forums
- degree of reuse of material in documentation
- satisfaction with training courses, newsletters, web briefings etc.

Acronyms

AMIS	Availability Management Information System
APMG	APM Group
BCM	Business Continuity Management
BCP	Business Continuity Plan
BCS	British Computer Society
BIA	Business Impact Analysis
BPO	Business Process Outsourcing
BU	Business Unit
CAB	Change Advisory Board
CCM	Component Capacity Management
CFIA	Component Failure Impact Analysis
CI	Configuration Item
CMDB	Configuration Management Database
CMIS	Capacity Management Information System
CMS	Configuration Management System
CS	Change Schedule
CSF	Critical Success Factor
CSI	Continual Service Improvement
CSP	Core Service Package
DIKW	Data Information Knowledge Wisdom
DML	Definitive Media Library
ECAB	Emergency Change Advisory Board
ELS	Early Life Support
FTA	Fault Tree Analysis
HR	Human Resources

ISMS	Information Security Management System
ITIL	Information Technology Infrastructure Library
ITSCM	IT Service Continuity Management
itSMF	IT Service Management Forum
KEDB	Known Error Database
KPI	Key Performance Indicator
KPO	Knowledge Process Outsourcing
LCS	Loyalist Certification Services
LOS	Line of Service
M_o_R	Management of Risk
MTBF	Mean Time Between Failures
MTBSI	Mean Time Between Service Incidents
MTTR	Mean Time To Repair
MTRS	Mean Time to Restore Service
OGC	Office of Government Commerce
OLA	Operational Level Agreement
PBA	Pattern of Business Activity
PDCA	Plan Do Check Act
PFS	Prerequisites for Success
PIR	Post-Implementation Review
PRINCE2	PRojects IN Controlled Environments
PSA	Projected Service Availability
PSO	Projected Service Outage
RAD	Rapid Application Development
RFC	Request for Change
SAC	Service Acceptance Criteria
SACM	Service Asset and Configuration Management
SCD	Supplier and Contract Database
SCM	Service Catalogue Management
SDP	Service Design Package
SFA	Service Failure Analysis
SIP	Service Improvement Plan
SKMS	Service Knowledge Management System
SLA	Service Level Agreement
SLM	Service Level Management
SLP	Service Level Package
SLR	Service Level Requirement
SOC	Separation of Concerns
SPM	Service Portfolio Management

SPOC	Single Point of Contact
SPOF	Single Point of Failure
TCU	Total Cost of Utilization
TSO	The Stationary Office
UC	Underpinning Contract
VBF	Vital Business Function
VCD	Variable Cost Dynamics

Glossary

Where a term is relevant to a particular phase in the Lifecycle of an IT Service, or to one of the Core ITIL publications, this is indicated at the beginning of the definition. This glossary is based on the official ITIL V3 Glossary, version 01 of 30 May 2007.

Acceptance	Formal agreement that an IT Service, Process, Plan, or other Deliverable is complete, accurate, Reliable and meets its specified Requirements. Acceptance is usually preceded by Evaluation or Testing and is often required before proceeding to the next stage of a Project or Process. See Service Acceptance Criteria.
Access Management	(Service Operation) The Process responsible for allowing Users to make use of IT Services, data, or other Assets. Access Management helps to protect the Confidentiality, Integrity and Availability of Assets by ensuring that only authorized Users are able to access or modify the Assets. Access Management is sometimes referred to as Rights Management or Identity Management.
Account Manager	(Service Strategy) A Role that is very similar to Business Relationship Manager, but includes more commercial aspects. Most commonly used when dealing with External Customers.
Accounting	(Service Strategy) The Process responsible for identifying actual Costs of delivering IT Services, comparing these with budgeted costs, and managing variance from the Budget.
Accredited	Officially authorized to carry out a Role. For example an Accredited body may be authorized to provide training or to conduct Audits.

Active Monitoring	(Service Operation) Monitoring of a Configuration Item or an IT Service that uses automated regular checks to discover the current status. See Passive Monitoring.
Activity	A set of actions designed to achieve a particular result. Activities are usually defined as part of Processes or Plans, and are documented in Procedures.
Agreed Service Time	(Service Design) A synonym for Service Hours, commonly used in formal calculations of Availability. See Downtime.
Agreement	A Document that describes a formal understanding between two or more parties. An Agreement is not legally binding, unless it forms part of a Contract. See Service Level Agreement, Operational Level Agreement.
Alert	(Service Operation) A warning that a threshold has been reached, something has changed, or a Failure has occurred. Alerts are often created and managed by System Management tools and are managed by the Event Management Process.
Analytical Modeling	(Service Strategy) (Service Design) (Continual Service Improvement) A technique that uses mathematical Models to predict the behavior of a Configuration Item or IT Service. Analytical Models are commonly used in Capacity Management and Availability Management. See Modeling.
Application	Software that provides Functions that are required by an IT Service. Each Application may be part of more than one IT Service. An Application runs on one or more Servers or Clients. See Application Management, Application Portfolio.
Application Management	(Service Design) (Service Operation) The Function responsible for managing Applications throughout their Lifecycle.
Application Portfolio	(Service Design) A database or structured Document used to manage Applications throughout their Lifecycle. The Application Portfolio contains key Attributes of all Applications. The Application Portfolio is sometimes implemented as part of the Service Portfolio, or as part of the Configuration Management System.
Application Service Provider (ASP)	(Service Design) An External Service Provider that provides IT Services using Applications running at the Service Provider's premises. Users access the Applications by network connections to the Service Provider.
Application Sizing	(Service Design) The Activity responsible for understanding the Resource Requirements needed to support a new Application, or a major Change to an existing Application. Application Sizing helps to ensure that the IT Service can meet its agreed Service Level Targets for Capacity and Performance.

Architecture   (Service Design) The structure of a System or IT Service, including the Relationships of Components to each other and to the environment they are in. Architecture also includes the Standards and Guidelines which guide the design and evolution of the System.

Assembly   (Service Transition) A Configuration Item that is made up from a number of other CIs. For example a Server CI may contain CIs for CPUs, Disks, Memory etc.; an IT Service CI may contain many Hardware, Software and other CIs.
                        See Component CI, Build.

Assessment   Inspection and analysis to check whether a Standard or set of Guidelines is being followed, that Records are accurate, or that Efficiency and Effectiveness targets are being met.
                        See Audit.

Asset   (Service Strategy) Any Resource or Capability. Assets of a Service Provider include anything that could contribute to the delivery of a Service. Assets can be one of the following types: Management, Organization, Process, Knowledge, People, Information, Applications, Infrastructure, and Financial Capital.

Asset Management   (Service Transition) Asset Management is the Process responsible for tracking and reporting the value and ownership of financial Assets throughout their Lifecycle. Asset Management is part of an overall Service Asset and Configuration Management Process.
                        See Asset Register.

Asset Register   (Service Transition) A list of Assets, which includes their ownership and value. The Asset Register is maintained by Asset Management.

Attribute   (Service Transition) A piece of information about a Configuration Item. Examples are name, location, Version number, and Cost. Attributes of CIs are recorded in the Configuration Management Database (CMDB).
                        See Relationship.

Audit   Formal inspection and verification to check whether a Standard or set of Guidelines is being followed, that Records are accurate, or that Efficiency and Effectiveness targets are being met. An Audit may be carried out by internal or external groups.
                        See Certification, Assessment.

Authority Matrix   Synonym for RACI.

Automatic Call   (Service Operation) Use of Information Technology to direct an incoming
Distribution (ACD)   telephone call to the most appropriate person in the shortest possible time. ACD is sometimes called Automated Call Distribution.

Availability	(Service Design) Ability of a Configuration Item or IT Service to perform its agreed Function when required. Availability is determined by Reliability, Maintainability, Serviceability, Performance, and Security. Availability is usually calculated as a percentage. This calculation is often based on Agreed Service Time and Downtime. It is Best Practice to calculate Availability using measurements of the Business output of the IT Service.
Availability Management	(Service Design) The Process responsible for defining, analyzing, Planning, measuring and improving all aspects of the Availability of IT Services. Availability Management is responsible for ensuring that all IT Infrastructure, Processes, Tools, Roles etc are appropriate for the agreed Service Level Targets for Availability.
Availability Management Information System (AMIS)	(Service Design) A virtual repository of all Availability Management data, usually stored in multiple physical locations. See Service Knowledge Management System.
Availability Plan	(Service Design) A Plan to ensure that existing and future Availability Requirements for IT Services can be provided Cost Effectively.
Back-out	Synonym for Remediation.
Backup	(Service Design) (Service Operation) Copying data to protect against loss of Integrity or Availability of the original.
Balanced Scorecard	(Continual Service Improvement) A management tool developed by Drs. Robert Kaplan (Harvard Business School) and David Norton. A Balanced Scorecard enables a Strategy to be broken down into Key Performance Indicators. Performance against the KPIs is used to demonstrate how well the Strategy is being achieved. A Balanced Scorecard has 4 major areas, each of which has a small number of KPIs. The same 4 areas are considered at different levels of detail throughout the Organization.
Baseline	(Continual Service Improvement) A Benchmark used as a reference point. For example: • An ITSM Baseline can be used as a starting point to measure the effect of a Service Improvement Plan • A Performance Baseline can be used to measure changes in Performance over the lifetime of an IT Service • A Configuration Management Baseline can be used to enable the IT Infrastructure to be restored to a known Configuration if a Change or Release fails
Benchmark	(Continual Service Improvement) The recorded state of something at a specific point in time. A Benchmark can be created for a Configuration, a Process, or any other set of data. For example, a benchmark can be used in: • Continual Service Improvement, to establish the current state for managing improvements. • Capacity Management, to document Performance characteristics during normal operations. • See Benchmarking, Baseline.

Benchmarking	(Continual Service Improvement) Comparing a Benchmark with a Baseline or with Best Practice. The term Benchmarking is also used to mean creating a series of Benchmarks over time, and comparing the results to measure progress or improvement.
Best Practice	Proven Activities or Processes that have been successfully used by multiple Organizations. ITIL is an example of Best Practice.
Brainstorming	(Service Design) A technique that helps a team to generate ideas. Ideas are not reviewed during the Brainstorming session, but at a later stage. Brainstorming is often used by Problem Management to identify possible causes.
British Standards Institution (BSI)	The UK National Standards body, responsible for creating and maintaining British Standards. See http://www.bsi-global.com for more information. See ISO.
Budget	A list of all the money an Organization or Business Unit plans to receive, and plans to pay out, over a specified period of time. See Budgeting, Planning.
Budgeting	The Activity of predicting and controlling the spending of money. Consists of a periodic negotiation cycle to set future Budgets (usually annual) and the day-to-day monitoring and adjusting of current Budgets.
Build	(Service Transition) The Activity of assembling a number of Configuration Items to create part of an IT Service. The term Build is also used to refer to a Release that is authorized for distribution. For example Server Build or laptop Build. See Configuration Baseline.
Build Environment	(Service Transition) A controlled Environment where Applications, IT Services and other Builds are assembled prior to being moved into a Test or Live Environment.
Business	(Service Strategy) An overall corporate entity or Organization formed of a number of Business Units. In the context of ITSM, the term Business includes public sector and not-for-profit organizations, as well as companies. An IT Service Provider provides IT Services to a Customer within a Business. The IT Service Provider may be part of the same Business as their Customer (Internal Service Provider), or part of another Business (External Service Provider).
Business Capacity Management (BCM)	(Service Design) In the context of ITSM, Business Capacity Management is the Activity responsible for understanding future Business Requirements for use in the Capacity Plan. See Service Capacity Management.

Business Case	(Service Strategy) Justification for a significant item of expenditure. Includes information about Costs, benefits, options, issues, Risks, and possible problems. See Cost Benefit Analysis.
Business Continuity Management (BCM)	(Service Design) The Business Process responsible for managing Risks that could seriously impact the Business. BCM safeguards the interests of key stakeholders, reputation, brand and value creating activities. The BCM Process involves reducing Risks to an acceptable level and planning for the recovery of Business Processes should a disruption to the Business occur. BCM sets the Objectives, Scope and Requirements for IT Service Continuity Management.
Business Continuity Plan (BCP)	(Service Design) A Plan defining the steps required to Restore Business Processes following a disruption. The Plan will also identify the triggers for Invocation, people to be involved, communications etc. IT Service Continuity Plans form a significant part of Business Continuity Plans.
Business Customer	(Service Strategy) A recipient of a product or a Service from the Business. For example if the Business is a car manufacturer then the Business Customer is someone who buys a car.
Business Impact Analysis (BIA)	(Service Strategy) BIA is the Activity in Business Continuity Management that identifies Vital Business Functions and their dependencies. These dependencies may include Suppliers, people, other Business Processes, IT Services etc. BIA defines the recovery requirements for IT Services. These requirements include Recovery Time Objectives, Recovery Point Objectives and minimum Service Level Targets for each IT Service.
Business Objective	(Service Strategy) The Objective of a Business Process, or of the Business as a whole. Business Objectives support the Business Vision, provide guidance for the IT Strategy, and are often supported by IT Services.
Business Operations	(Service Strategy) The day-to-day execution, monitoring and management of Business Processes.
Business Perspective	(Continual Service Improvement) An understanding of the Service Provider and IT Services from the point of view of the Business, and an understanding of the Business from the point of view of the Service Provider.
Business Process	A Process that is owned and carried out by the Business. A Business Process contributes to the delivery of a product or Service to a Business Customer. For example, a retailer may have a purchasing Process which helps to deliver Services to their Business Customers. Many Business Processes rely on IT Services.

Business Relationship Management	(Service Strategy) The Process or Function responsible for maintaining a Relationship with the Business. BRM usually includes:

Business Relationship Management

(Service Strategy) The Process or Function responsible for maintaining a Relationship with the Business. BRM usually includes:
- Managing personal Relationships with Business managers
- Providing input to Service Portfolio Management
- Ensuring that the IT Service Provider is satisfying the Business needs of the Customers

This Process has strong links with Service Level Management.

Business Relationship Manager (BRM)

(Service Strategy) A Role responsible for maintaining the Relationship with one or more Customers. This Role is often combined with the Service Level Manager Role.
See Account Manager.

Business Service

An IT Service that directly supports a Business Process, as opposed to an Infrastructure Service which is used internally by the IT Service Provider and is not usually visible to the Business.
The term Business Service is also used to mean a Service that is delivered to Business Customers by Business Units. For example delivery of financial services to Customers of a bank, or goods to the Customers of a retail store. Successful delivery of Business Services often depends on one or more IT Services.

Business Service Management (BSM)

(Service Strategy) (Service Design) An approach to the management of IT Services that considers the Business Processes supported and the Business value provided.
This term also means the management of Business Services delivered to Business Customers.

Business Unit

(Service Strategy) A segment of the Business which has its own Plans, Metrics, income and Costs. Each Business Unit owns Assets and uses these to create value for Customers in the form of goods and Services.

Call

(Service Operation) A telephone call to the Service Desk from a User. A Call could result in an Incident or a Service Request being logged.

Call Centre

(Service Operation) An Organization or Business Unit which handles large numbers of incoming and outgoing telephone calls.
See Service Desk.

Call Type

(Service Operation) A Category that is used to distinguish incoming requests to a Service Desk. Common Call Types are Incident, Service Request and Complaint.

Capability

(Service Strategy) The ability of an Organization, person, Process, Application, Configuration Item or IT Service to carry out an Activity. Capabilities are intangible Assets of an Organization.
See Resource.

Capability Maturity Model (CMM)	(Continual Service Improvement) The Capability Maturity Model for Software (also known as the CMM and SW-CMM) is a model used to identify Best Practices to help increase Process Maturity. CMM was developed at the Software Engineering Institute (SEI) of Carnegie Mellon University. In 2000, the SW-CMM was upgraded to CMMI® (Capability Maturity Model Integration). The SEI no longer maintains the SW-CMM model, its associated appraisal methods, or training materials.
Capability Maturity Model Integration (CMMI)	(Continual Service Improvement) Capability Maturity Model® Integration (CMMI) is a process improvement approach developed by the Software Engineering Institute (SEI) of Carnegie Melon University. CMMI provides organizations with the essential elements of effective processes. It can be used to guide process improvement across a project, a division, or an entire organization. CMMI helps integrate traditionally separate organizational functions, set process improvement goals and priorities, provide guidance for quality processes, and provide a point of reference for appraising current processes. See http://www.sei.cmu.edu/cmmi/ for more information. See CMM, Continuous Improvement, Maturity.
Capacity	(Service Design) The maximum Throughput that a Configuration Item or IT Service can deliver whilst meeting agreed Service Level Targets. For some types of CI, Capacity may be the size or volume, for example a disk drive.
Capacity Management	(Service Design) The Process responsible for ensuring that the Capacity of IT Services and the IT Infrastructure is able to deliver agreed Service Level Targets in a Cost Effective and timely manner. Capacity Management considers all Resources required to deliver the IT Service, and plans for short, medium and long term Business Requirements.
Capacity Management Information System (CMIS)	(Service Design) A virtual repository of all Capacity Management data, usually stored in multiple physical locations. See Service Knowledge Management System.
Capacity Plan	(Service Design) A Capacity Plan is used to manage the Resources required to deliver IT Services. The Plan contains scenarios for different predictions of Business demand, and costed options to deliver the agreed Service Level Targets.
Capacity Planning	(Service Design) The Activity within Capacity Management responsible for creating a Capacity Plan.
Capital Expenditure (CAPEX)	(Service Strategy) The Cost of purchasing something that will become a financial Asset, for example computer equipment and buildings. The value of the Asset is Depreciated over multiple accounting periods.
Capital Item	(Service Strategy) An Asset that is of interest to Financial Management because it is above an agreed financial value.

Capitalization	(Service Strategy) Identifying major Cost as capital, even though no Asset is purchased. This is done to spread the impact of the Cost over multiple accounting periods. The most common example of this is software development, or purchase of a software license.
Category	A named group of things that have something in common. Categories are used to group similar things together. For example Cost Types are used to group similar types of Cost. Incident Categories are used to group similar types of Incident, CI Types are used to group similar types of Configuration Item.
Certification	Issuing a certificate to confirm Compliance to a Standard. Certification includes a formal Audit by an independent and Accredited body. The term Certification is also used to mean awarding a certificate to verify that a person has achieved a qualification.
Change	(Service Transition) The addition, modification or removal of anything that could have an effect on IT Services. The Scope should include all IT Services, Configuration Items, Processes, Documentation etc.
Change Advisory Board (CAB)	(Service Transition) A group of people that advises the Change Manager in the Assessment, prioritization and scheduling of Changes. This board is usually made up of representatives from all areas within the IT Service Provider, the Business, and Third Parties such as Suppliers.
Change Case	(Service Operation) A technique used to predict the impact of proposed Changes. Change Cases use specific scenarios to clarify the scope of proposed Changes and to help with Cost Benefit Analysis. See Use Case.
Change History	(Service Transition) Information about all changes made to a Configuration Item during its life. Change History consists of all those Change Records that apply to the CI.
Change Management	(Service Transition) The Process responsible for controlling the Lifecycle of all Changes. The primary objective of Change Management is to enable beneficial Changes to be made, with minimum disruption to IT Services.
Change Model	(Service Transition) A repeatable way of dealing with a particular Category of Change. A Change Model defines specific pre-defined steps that will be followed for a Change of this Category. Change Models may be very simple, with no requirement for approval (e.g. Password Reset) or may be very complex with many steps that require approval (e.g. major software Release). See Standard Change, Change Advisory Board.

Change Record	(Service Transition) A Record containing the details of a Change. Each Change Record documents the Lifecycle of a single Change. A Change Record is created for every Request for Change that is received, even those that are subsequently rejected. Change Records should reference the Configuration Items that are affected by the Change. Change Records are stored in the Configuration Management System.
Change Request	Synonym for Request for Change.
Change Schedule	(Service Transition) A Document that lists all approved Changes and their planned implementation dates. A Change Schedule is sometimes called a Forward Schedule of Change, even though it also contains information about Changes that have already been implemented.
Change Window	(Service Transition) A regular, agreed time when Changes or Releases may be implemented with minimal impact on Services. Change Windows are usually documented in SLAs.
Charging	(Service Strategy) Requiring payment for IT Services. Charging for IT Services is optional, and many Organizations choose to treat their IT Service Provider as a Cost Centre.
Chronological Analysis	(Service Operation) A technique used to help identify possible causes of Problems. All available data about the Problem is collected and sorted by date and time to provide a detailed timeline. This can make it possible to identify which Events may have been triggered by others.
CI Type	(Service Transition) A Category that is used to Classify CIs. The CI Type identifies the required Attributes and Relationships for a Configuration Record. Common CI Types include: hardware, Document, User etc.
Classification	The act of assigning a Category to something. Classification is used to ensure consistent management and reporting. CIs, Incidents, Problems, Changes etc. are usually classified.
Client	A generic term that means a Customer, the Business or a Business Customer. For example Client Manager may be used as a synonym for Account Manager. The term client is also used to mean: • A computer that is used directly by a User, for example a PC, Handheld Computer, or Workstation. • The part of a Client-Server Application that the User directly interfaces with. For example an email Client.
Closed	(Service Operation) The final Status in the Lifecycle of an Incident, Problem, Change etc. When the Status is Closed, no further action is taken.
Closure	(Service Operation) The act of changing the Status of an Incident, Problem, Change etc. to Closed.

CobiT	(Continual Service Improvement) Control Objectives for Information and related Technology (CobiT) provides guidance and Best Practice for the management of IT Processes. CobiT is published by the IT Governance Institute. See http://www.isaca.org/ for more information.
Code of Practice	A Guideline published by a public body or a Standards Organization, such as ISO or BSI. Many Standards consist of a Code of Practice and a Specification. The Code of Practice describes recommended Best Practice.
Cold Standby	Synonym for Gradual Recovery.
Commercial off the Shelf (COTS)	(Service Design) Application software or Middleware that can be purchased from a Third Party.
Compliance	Ensuring that a Standard or set of Guidelines is followed, or that proper, consistent accounting or other practices are being employed.
Component	A general term that is used to mean one part of something more complex. For example, a computer System may be a component of an IT Service, an Application may be a Component of a Release Unit. Components that need to be managed should be Configuration Items.
Component Capacity Management (CCM)	(Service Design) (Continual Service Improvement) The Process responsible for understanding the Capacity, Utilization, and Performance of Configuration Items. Data is collected, recorded and analyzed for use in the Capacity Plan. See Service Capacity Management.
Component CI	(Service Transition) A Configuration Item that is part of an Assembly. For example, a CPU or Memory CI may be part of a Server CI.
Component Failure Impact Analysis (CFIA)	(Service Design) A technique that helps to identify the impact of CI failure on IT Services. A matrix is created with IT Services on one edge and CIs on the other. This enables the identification of critical CIs (that could cause the failure of multiple IT Services) and of fragile IT Services (that have multiple Single Points of Failure).
Computer Telephony Integration (CTI)	(Service Operation) CTI is a general term covering any kind of integration between computers and telephone Systems. It is most commonly used to refer to Systems where an Application displays detailed screens relating to incoming or outgoing telephone calls. See Automatic Call Distribution, Interactive Voice Response.
Concurrency	A measure of the number of Users engaged in the same Operation at the same time.
Confidentiality	(Service Design) A security principle that requires that data should only be accessed by authorized people.

Configuration	(Service Transition) A generic term, used to describe a group of Configuration Items that work together to deliver an IT Service, or a recognizable part of an IT Service. Configuration is also used to describe the parameter settings for one or more CIs.
Configuration Baseline	(Service Transition) A Baseline of a Configuration that has been formally agreed and is managed through the Change Management process. A Configuration Baseline is used as a basis for future Builds, Releases and Changes.
Configuration Control	(Service Transition) The Activity responsible for ensuring that adding, modifying or removing a CI is properly managed, for example by submitting a Request for Change or Service Request.
Configuration Identification	(Service Transition) The Activity responsible for collecting information about Configuration Items and their Relationships, and loading this information into the CMDB. Configuration Identification is also responsible for labeling the CIs themselves, so that the corresponding Configuration Records can be found.
Configuration Item (CI)	(Service Transition) Any Component that needs to be managed in order to deliver an IT Service. Information about each CI is recorded in a Configuration Record within the Configuration Management System and is maintained throughout its Lifecycle by Configuration Management. CIs are under the control of Change Management. CIs typically include IT Services, hardware, software, buildings, people, and formal documentation such as Process documentation and SLAs.
Configuration Management	(Service Transition) The Process responsible for maintaining information about Configuration Items required to deliver an IT Service, including their Relationships. This information is managed throughout the Lifecycle of the CI. Configuration Management is part of an overall Service Asset and Configuration Management Process.
Configuration Management Database (CMDB)	(Service Transition) A database used to store Configuration Records throughout their Lifecycle. The Configuration Management System maintains one or more CMDBs, and each CMDB stores Attributes of CIs, and Relationships with other CIs.
Configuration Management System (CMS)	(Service Transition) A set of tools and databases that are used to manage an IT Service Provider's Configuration data. The CMS also includes information about Incidents, Problems, Known Errors, Changes and Releases; and may contain data about employees, Suppliers, locations, Business Units, Customers and Users. The CMS includes tools for collecting, storing, managing, updating, and presenting data about all Configuration Items and their Relationships. The CMS is maintained by Configuration Management and is used by all IT Service Management Processes. See Configuration Management Database, Service Knowledge Management System.

Configuration Record	(Service Transition) A Record containing the details of a Configuration Item. Each Configuration Record documents the Lifecycle of a single CI. Configuration Records are stored in a Configuration Management Database.
Configuration Structure	(Service Transition) The hierarchy and other Relationships between all the Configuration Items that comprise a Configuration.
Continual Service Improvement (CSI)	(Continual Service Improvement) A stage in the Lifecycle of an IT Service and the title of one of the Core ITIL publications. Continual Service Improvement is responsible for managing improvements to IT Service Management Processes and IT Services. The Performance of the IT Service Provider is continually measured and improvements are made to Processes, IT Services and IT Infrastructure in order to increase Efficiency, Effectiveness, and Cost Effectiveness. See Plan-Do-Check-Act.
Continuous Availability	(Service Design) An approach or design to achieve 100% Availability. A Continuously Available IT Service has no planned or unplanned Downtime.
Continuous Operation	(Service Design) An approach or design to eliminate planned Downtime of an IT Service. Note that individual Configuration Items may be down even though the IT Service is Available.
Contract	A legally binding Agreement between two or more parties.
Contract Portfolio	(Service Strategy) A database or structured Document used to manage Service Contracts or Agreements between an IT Service Provider and their Customers. Each IT Service delivered to a Customer should have a Contract or other Agreement which is listed in the Contract Portfolio. See Service Portfolio, Service Catalogue.
Control	A means of managing a Risk, ensuring that a Business Objective is achieved, or ensuring that a Process is followed. Example Controls include Policies, Procedures, Roles, RAID, door-locks etc. A control is sometimes called a Countermeasure or safeguard. Control also means to manage the utilization or behavior of a Configuration Item, System or IT Service.
Control Objectives for Information and related Technology (COBIT)	See COBIT.
Control perspective	(Service Strategy) An approach to the management of IT Services, Processes, Functions, Assets etc. There can be several different Control Perspectives on the same IT Service, Process etc., allowing different individuals or teams to focus on what is important and relevant to their specific Role. Example Control Perspectives include Reactive and Proactive management within IT Operations, or a Lifecycle view for an Application Project team.

Control Processes	The ISO/IEC 20000 Process group that includes Change Management and Configuration Management.
Core Service	(Service Strategy) An IT Service that delivers basic Outcomes desired by one or more Customers. See Supporting Service, Core Service Package.
Core Service Package (CSP)	(Service Strategy) A detailed description of a Core Service that may be shared by two or more Service Level Packages. See Service Package.
Cost	The amount of money spent on a specific Activity, IT Service, or Business Unit. Costs consist of real cost (money), notional cost such as people's time, and Depreciation.
Cost Benefit Analysis	An Activity that analyses and compares the Costs and the benefits involved in one or more alternative courses of action. See Business Case, Net Present Value, Internal Rate of Return, Return on Investment, Value on Investment.
Cost Centre	(Service Strategy) A Business Unit or Project to which Costs are assigned. A Cost Centre does not charge for Services provided. An IT Service Provider can be run as a Cost Centre or a Profit Centre.
Cost Effectiveness	A measure of the balance between the Effectiveness and Cost of a Service, Process or activity, A Cost Effective Process is one which achieves its Objectives at minimum Cost. See KPI, Return on Investment, Value for Money.
Cost Element	(Service Strategy) The middle level of category to which Costs are assigned in Budgeting and Accounting. The highest level category is Cost Type. For example a Cost Type of "people" could have cost elements of payroll, staff benefits, expenses, training, overtime etc. Cost Elements can be further broken down to give Cost Units. For example the Cost Element "expenses" could include Cost Units of Hotels, Transport, Meals etc.
Cost Management	(Service Strategy) A general term that is used to refer to Budgeting and Accounting, sometimes used as a synonym for Financial Management
Cost Type	(Service Strategy) The highest level of category to which Costs are assigned in Budgeting and Accounting. For example hardware, software, people, accommodation, external and Transfer. See Cost Element, Cost Type.
Cost Unit	(Service Strategy) The lowest level of category to which Costs are assigned, Cost Units are usually things that can be easily counted (e.g. staff numbers, software licenses) or things easily measured (e.g. CPU usage, Electricity consumed). Cost Units are included within Cost Elements. For example a Cost Element of "expenses" could include Cost Units of Hotels, Transport, Meals etc. See Cost Type.

Countermeasure	Can be used to refer to any type of Control. The term Countermeasure is most often used when referring to measures that increase Resilience, Fault Tolerance or Reliability of an IT Service.
Course Corrections	Changes made to a Plan or Activity that has already started, to ensure that it will meet its Objectives. Course corrections are made as a result of Monitoring progress.
CRAMM	A methodology and tool for analyzing and managing Risks. CRAMM was developed by the UK Government, but is now privately owned. Further information is available from http://www.cramm.com/
Crisis Management	The Process responsible for managing the wider implications of Business Continuity. A Crisis Management team is responsible for Strategic issues such as managing media relations and shareholder confidence, and decides when to invoke Business Continuity Plans.
Critical Success Factor (CSF)	Something that must happen if a Process, Project, Plan, or IT Service is to succeed. KPIs are used to measure the achievement of each CSF. For example a CSF of "protect IT Services when making Changes" could be measured by KPIs such as "percentage reduction of unsuccessful Changes", "percentage reduction in Changes causing Incidents" etc.
Culture	A set of values that is shared by a group of people, including expectations about how people should behave, ideas, beliefs, and practices. See Vision.
Customer	Someone who buys goods or Services. The Customer of an IT Service Provider is the person or group who defines and agrees the Service Level Targets. The term Customers is also sometimes informally used to mean Users, for example "this is a Customer focused Organization".
Customer Portfolio	(Service Strategy) A database or structured Document used to record all Customers of the IT Service Provider. The Customer Portfolio is the Business Relationship Manager's view of the Customers who receive Services from the IT Service Provider. See Contract Portfolio, Service Portfolio.
Dashboard	(Service Operation) A graphical representation of overall IT Service Performance and Availability. Dashboard images may be updated in real-time, and can also be included in management reports and web pages. Dashboards can be used to support Service Level Management, Event Management or Incident Diagnosis.
Data-to-Information-to-Knowledge-to-Wisdom (DIKW)	A way of understanding the relationships between data, information, knowledge, and wisdom. DIKW shows how each of these builds on the others.

Definitive Media Library (DML)	(Service Transition) One or more locations in which the definitive and approved versions of all software Configuration Items are securely stored. The DML may also contain associated CIs such as licenses and documentation. The DML is a single logical storage area even if there are multiple locations. All software in the DML is under the control of Change and Release Management and is recorded in the Configuration Management System. Only software from the DML is acceptable for use in a Release.
Deliverable	Something that must be provided to meet a commitment in a Service Level Agreement or a Contract. Deliverable is also used in a more informal way to mean a planned output of any Process.
Demand Management	Activities that understand and influence Customer demand for Services and the provision of Capacity to meet these demands. At a Strategic level Demand Management can involve analysis of Patterns of Business Activity and User Profiles. At a Tactical level it can involve use of Differential Charging to encourage Customers to use IT Services at less busy times. See Capacity Management.
Deming Cycle	Synonym for Plan Do Check Act.
Dependency	The direct or indirect reliance of one Process or Activity upon another.
Deployment	(Service Transition) The Activity responsible for movement of new or changed hardware, software, documentation, Process, etc to the Live Environment. Deployment is part of the Release and Deployment Management Process. See Rollout.
Depreciation	(Service Strategy) A measure of the reduction in value of an Asset over its life. This is based on wearing out, consumption or other reduction in the useful economic value.
Design	(Service Design) An Activity or Process that identifies Requirements and then defines a solution that is able to meet these Requirements. See Service Design.
Detection	(Service Operation) A stage in the Incident Lifecycle. Detection results in the Incident becoming known to the Service Provider. Detection can be automatic, or can be the result of a User logging an Incident.
Development	(Service Design) The Process responsible for creating or modifying an IT Service or Application. Also used to mean the Role or group that carries out Development work.
Development Environment	(Service Design) An Environment used to create or modify IT Services or Applications. Development Environments are not typically subjected to the same degree of control as Test Environments or Live Environments. See Development.

Diagnosis

(Service Operation) A stage in the Incident and Problem Lifecycles. The purpose of Diagnosis is to identify a Workaround for an Incident or the Root Cause of a Problem.

Diagnostic Script

(Service Operation) A structured set of questions used by Service Desk staff to ensure they ask the correct questions, and to help them Classify, Resolve and assign Incidents. Diagnostic Scripts may also be made available to Users to help them diagnose and resolve their own Incidents.

Differential Charging

A technique used to support Demand Management by charging different amounts for the same IT Service Function at different times.

Direct Cost

(Service Strategy) A cost of providing an IT Service which can be allocated in full to a specific Customer, Cost Centre, Project etc. For example cost of providing non-shared servers or software licenses.
See Indirect Cost.

Directory Service

(Service Operation) An Application that manages information about IT Infrastructure available on a network, and corresponding User access Rights.

Do Nothing

(Service Design) A Recovery Option. The Service Provider formally agrees with the Customer that Recovery of this IT Service will not be performed.

Document

Information in readable form. A Document may be paper or electronic. For example a Policy statement, Service Level Agreement, Incident Record, diagram of computer room layout.
See Record.

Downtime

(Service Design) (Service Operation) The time when a Configuration Item or IT Service is not Available during its Agreed Service Time. The Availability of an IT Service is often calculated from Agreed Service Time and Downtime.

Driver

Something that influences Strategy, Objectives or Requirements. For example new legislation or the actions of competitors.

Early Life Support

(Service Transition) Support provided for a new or Changed IT Service for a period of time after it is Released. During Early Life Support the IT Service Provider may review the KPIs, Service Levels and Monitoring Thresholds, and provide additional Resources for Incident and Problem Management.

Economies of scale

(Service Strategy) The reduction in average Cost that is possible from increasing the usage of an IT Service or Asset.
See Economies of Scope.

Economies of scope

(Service Strategy) The reduction in Cost that is allocated to an IT Service by using an existing Asset for an additional purpose. For example delivering a new IT Service from existing IT Infrastructure.
See Economies of Scale.

Effectiveness	(Continual Service Improvement) A measure of whether the Objectives of a Process, Service or Activity have been achieved. An Effective Process or Activity is one that achieves its agreed Objectives. See KPI.
Efficiency	(Continual Service Improvement) A measure of whether the right amount of resources have been used to deliver a Process, Service or Activity. An Efficient Process achieves its Objectives with the minimum amount of time, money, people or other resources. See KPI.
Emergency Change	(Service Transition) A Change that must be introduced as soon as possible. For example to resolve a Major Incident or implement a Security patch. The Change Management Process will normally have a specific Procedure for handling Emergency Changes. See Emergency Change Advisory Board (ECAB).
Emergency Change Advisory Board (ECAB)	(Service Transition) A sub-set of the Change Advisory Board who make decisions about high impact Emergency Changes. Membership of the ECAB may be decided at the time a meeting is called, and depends on the nature of the Emergency Change.
Environment	(Service Transition) A subset of the IT Infrastructure that is used for a particular purpose. For Example: Live Environment, Test Environment, Build Environment. It is possible for multiple Environments to share a Configuration Item, for example Test and Live Environments may use different partitions on a single mainframe computer. Also used in the term Physical Environment to mean the accommodation, air conditioning, power system etc. Environment is also used as a generic term to mean the external conditions that influence or affect something.
Error	(Service Operation) A design flaw or malfunction that causes a Failure of one or more Configuration Items or IT Services. A mistake made by a person or a faulty Process that impacts a CI or IT Service is also an Error.
Escalation	(Service Operation) An Activity that obtains additional Resources when these are needed to meet Service Level Targets or Customer expectations. Escalation may be needed within any IT Service Management Process, but is most commonly associated with Incident Management, Problem Management and the management of Customer complaints. There are two types of Escalation, Functional Escalation and Hierarchic Escalation.
eSourcing Capability Model for Client Organizations (eSCM-CL)	(Service Strategy) A framework to help Organizations guide their analysis and decisions on Service Sourcing Models and Strategies. eSCM-CL was developed by Carnegie Mellon University. See eSCM-SP.

eSourcing Capability Model for Service Providers (eSCM-SP)	(Service Strategy) A framework to help IT Service Providers develop their IT Service Management Capabilities from a Service Sourcing perspective. eSCM-SP was developed by Carnegie Mellon University. See eSCM-CL.
Estimation	The use of experience to provide an approximate value for a Metric or Cost. Estimation is also used in Capacity and Availability Management as the cheapest and least accurate Modeling method.
Evaluation	(Service Transition) The Process responsible for assessing a new or Changed IT Service to ensure that Risks have been managed and to help determine whether to proceed with the Change. Evaluation is also used to mean comparing an actual Outcome with the intended Outcome, or comparing one alternative with another.
Event	(Service Operation) A change of state which has significance for the management of a Configuration Item or IT Service. The term Event is also used to mean an Alert or notification created by any IT Service, Configuration Item or Monitoring tool. Events typically require IT Operations personnel to take actions, and often lead to Incidents being logged.
Event Management	(Service Operation) The Process responsible for managing Events throughout their Lifecycle. Event Management is one of the main Activities of IT Operations.
Exception Report	A Document containing details of one or more KPIs or other important targets that have exceeded defined Thresholds. Examples include SLA targets being missed or about to be missed, and a Performance Metric indicating a potential Capacity problem.
Expanded Incident Lifecycle	(Availability Management) Detailed stages in the Lifecycle of an Incident. The stages are Detection, Diagnosis, Repair, Recovery, Restoration. The Expanded Incident Lifecycle is used to help understand all contributions to the Impact of Incidents and to Plan how these could be controlled or reduced.
External Customer	A Customer who works for a different Business to the IT Service Provider. See External Service Provider, Internal Customer.
External Metric	A Metric that is used to measure the delivery of IT Service to a Customer. External Metrics are usually defined in SLAs and reported to Customers. See Internal Metric.
External Service Provider	(Service Strategy) An IT Service Provider which is part of a different Organization to their Customer. An IT Service Provider may have both Internal Customers and External Customers. See Type III Service Provider.
External Sourcing	Synonym for Outsourcing.

Facilities Management	(Service Operation) The Function responsible for managing the physical Environment where the IT Infrastructure is located. Facilities Management includes all aspects of managing the physical Environment, for example power and cooling, building Access Management, and environmental Monitoring.
Failure	(Service Operation) Loss of ability to Operate to Specification, or to deliver the required output. The term Failure may be used when referring to IT Services, Processes, Activities, Configuration Items etc. A Failure often causes an Incident.
Failure Modes and Effects Analysis (FMEA)	An approach to assessing the potential Impact of Failures. FMEA involves analyzing what would happen after Failure of each Configuration Item, all the way up to the effect on the Business. FMEA is often used in Information Security Management and in IT Service Continuity Planning.
Fast Recovery	(Service Design) A Recovery Option which is also known as Hot Standby. Provision is made to Recover the IT Service in a short period of time, typically less than 24 hours. Fast Recovery typically uses a dedicated Fixed Facility with computer Systems, and software configured ready to run the IT Services. Immediate Recovery may take up to 24 hours if there is a need to Restore data from Backups.
Fault	Synonym for Error.
Fault Tolerance	(Service Design) The ability of an IT Service or Configuration Item to continue to Operate correctly after Failure of a Component part. See Resilience, Countermeasure.
Fault Tree Analysis (FTA)	(Service Design) (Continual Service Improvement) A technique that can be used to determine the chain of Events that leads to a Problem. Fault Tree Analysis represents a chain of Events using Boolean notation in a diagram.
Financial Management	(Service Strategy) The Function and Processes responsible for managing an IT Service Provider's Budgeting, Accounting and Charging Requirements.
First-line Support	(Service Operation) The first level in a hierarchy of Support Groups involved in the resolution of Incidents. Each level contains more specialist skills, or has more time or other Resources. See Escalation.
Fishbone Diagram	Synonym for Ishikawa Diagram.
Fit for Purpose	An informal term used to describe a Process, Configuration Item, IT Service etc. that is capable of meeting its Objectives or Service Levels. Being Fit for Purpose requires suitable Design, implementation, Control and maintenance.
Fixed Cost	(Service Strategy) A Cost that does not vary with IT Service usage. For example the cost of Server hardware. See Variable Cost.

Fixed Facility	(Service Design) A permanent building, available for use when needed by an IT Service Continuity Plan. See Recovery Option, Portable Facility.
Follow the Sun	(Service Operation) A methodology for using Service Desks and Support Groups around the world to provide seamless 24 * 7 Service. Calls, Incidents, Problems and Service Requests are passed between groups in different time zones.
Fulfilment	Performing Activities to meet a need or Requirement. For example by providing a new IT Service, or meeting a Service Request.
Function	A team or group of people and the tools they use to carry out one or more Processes or Activities. For example the Service Desk. The term Function also has two other meanings • An intended purpose of a Configuration Item, Person, Team, Process, or IT Service. For example one Function of an Email Service may be to store and forward outgoing mails, one Function of a Business Process may be to dispatch goods to Customers. • To perform the intended purpose correctly, "The computer is Functioning"
Functional Escalation	(Service Operation) Transferring an Incident, Problem or Change to a technical team with a higher level of expertise to assist in an Escalation.
Gap Analysis	(Continual Service Improvement) An Activity which compares two sets of data and identifies the differences. Gap Analysis is commonly used to compare a set of Requirements with actual delivery. See Benchmarking.
Governance	Ensuring that Policies and Strategy are actually implemented, and that required Processes are correctly followed. Governance includes defining Roles and responsibilities, measuring and reporting, and taking actions to resolve any issues identified.
Gradual Recovery	(Service Design) A Recovery Option which is also known as Cold Standby. Provision is made to Recover the IT Service in a period of time greater than 72 hours. Gradual Recovery typically uses a Portable or Fixed Facility that has environmental support and network cabling, but no computer Systems. The hardware and software are installed as part of the IT Service Continuity Plan.
Guideline	A Document describing Best Practice, that recommends what should be done. Compliance to a guideline is not normally enforced. See Standard.
Help Desk	(Service Operation) A point of contact for Users to log Incidents. A Help Desk is usually more technically focused than a Service Desk and does not provide a Single Point of Contact for all interaction. The term Help Desk is often used as a synonym for Service Desk.

Hierarchic Escalation	(Service Operation) Informing or involving more senior levels of management to assist in an Escalation.
High Availability	(Service Design) An approach or Design that minimizes or hides the effects of Configuration Item Failure on the Users of an IT Service. High Availability solutions are Designed to achieve an agreed level of Availability and make use of techniques such as Fault Tolerance, Resilience and fast Recovery to reduce the number of Incidents, and the Impact of Incidents.
Hot Standby	Synonym for Fast Recovery or Immediate Recovery.
Identity	(Service Operation) A unique name that is used to identify a User, person or Role. The Identity is used to grant Rights to that User, person, or Role. Example identities might be the username SmithJ or the Role "Change manager".
Immediate Recovery	(Service Design) A Recovery Option which is also known as Hot Standby. Provision is made to Recover the IT Service with no loss of Service. Immediate Recovery typically uses mirroring, load balancing and split site technologies.
Impact	(Service Operation) (Service Transition) A measure of the effect of an Incident, Problem or Change on Business Processes. Impact is often based on how Service Levels will be affected. Impact and Urgency are used to assign Priority.
Incident	(Service Operation) An unplanned interruption to an IT Service or a reduction in the Quality of an IT Service. Failure of a Configuration Item that has not yet impacted Service is also an Incident. For example Failure of one disk from a mirror set.
Incident Management	(Service Operation) The Process responsible for managing the Lifecycle of all Incidents. The primary Objective of Incident Management is to return the IT Service to Users as quickly as possible.
Incident Record	(Service Operation) A Record containing the details of an Incident. Each Incident record documents the Lifecycle of a single Incident.
Indirect Cost	(Service Strategy) A Cost of providing an IT Service which cannot be allocated in full to a specific Customer. For example Cost of providing shared Servers or software licenses. Also known as Overhead. See Direct Cost.
Information Security Management (ISM)	(Service Design) The Process that ensures the Confidentiality, Integrity and Availability of an Organization's Assets, information, data and IT Services. Information Security Management usually forms part of an Organizational approach to Security Management which has a wider scope than the IT Service Provider, and includes handling of paper, building access, phone calls etc., for the entire Organization.

Information Security Management System (ISMS)	(Service Design) The framework of Policy, Processes, Standards, Guidelines and tools that ensures an Organization can achieve its Information Security Management Objectives.
Information Security Policy	(Service Design) The Policy that governs the Organization's approach to Information Security Management.
Information Technology (IT)	The use of technology for the storage, communication or processing of information. The technology typically includes computers, telecommunications, Applications and other software. The information may include Business data, voice, images, video, etc. Information Technology is often used to support Business Processes through IT Services.
Infrastructure Service	An IT Service that is not directly used by the Business, but is required by the IT Service Provider so they can provide other IT Services. For example Directory Services, naming services, or communication services.
Insourcing	Synonym for Internal Sourcing.
Integrity	(Service Design) A security principle that ensures data and Configuration Items are only modified by authorized personnel and Activities. Integrity considers all possible causes of modification, including software and hardware Failure, environmental Events, and human intervention.
Interactive Voice Response (IVR)	(Service Operation) A form of Automatic Call Distribution that accepts User input, such as key presses and spoken commands, to identify the correct destination for incoming Calls.
Intermediate Recovery	(Service Design) A Recovery Option which is also known as Warm Standby. Provision is made to Recover the IT Service in a period of time between 24 and 72 hours. Intermediate Recovery typically uses a shared Portable or Fixed Facility that has computer Systems and network Components. The hardware and software will need to be configured, and data will need to be restored, as part of the IT Service Continuity Plan.
Internal Customer	A Customer who works for the same Business as the IT Service Provider. See Internal Service Provider, External Customer.
Internal Metric	A Metric that is used within the IT Service Provider to Monitor the Efficiency, Effectiveness or Cost Effectiveness of the IT Service Provider's internal Processes. Internal Metrics are not normally reported to the Customer of the IT Service. See External Metric.
Internal Rate of Return (IRR)	(Service Strategy) A technique used to help make decisions about Capital Expenditure. IRR calculates a figure that allows two or more alternative investments to be compared. A larger IRR indicates a better investment. See Net Present Value, Return on Investment.
Internal Service Provider	(Service Strategy) An IT Service Provider which is part of the same Organization as their Customer. An IT Service Provider may have both Internal Customers and External Customers. See Type I Service Provider, Type II Service Provider, Insource.

Internal Sourcing	(Service Strategy) Using an Internal Service Provider to manage IT Services. See Service Sourcing, Type I Service Provider, Type II Service Provider.
International Organization for Standardization (ISO)	The International Organization for Standardization (ISO) is the world's largest developer of Standards. ISO is a non-governmental organization which is a network of the national standards institutes of 156 countries. Further information about ISO is available from http://www.iso.org/
International Standards Organization	See International Organization for Standardization (ISO)
Internet Service Provider (ISP)	An External Service Provider that provides access to the Internet. Most ISPs also provide other IT Services such as web hosting.
Invocation	(Service Design) Initiation of the steps defined in a plan. For example initiating the IT Service Continuity Plan for one or more IT Services.
Ishikawa Diagram	(Service Operation) (Continual Service Improvement) A technique that helps a team to identify all the possible causes of a Problem. Originally devised by Kaoru Ishikawa, the output of this technique is a diagram that looks like a fishbone.
ISO 9000	A generic term that refers to a number of international Standards and Guidelines for Quality Management Systems. See http://www.iso.org/ for more information. See ISO.
ISO 9001	An international Standard for Quality Management Systems. See ISO 9000, Standard.
ISO/IEC 17799	(Continual Service Improvement) ISO Code of Practice for Information Security Management. See Standard.
ISO/IEC 20000	ISO Specification and Code of Practice for IT Service Management. ISO/IEC 20000 is aligned with ITIL Best Practice.
ISO/IEC 27001	(Service Design) (Continual Service Improvement) ISO Specification for Information Security Management. The corresponding Code of Practice is ISO/IEC 17799. See Standard.
IT Directorate	(Continual Service Improvement) Senior Management within a Service Provider, charged with developing and delivering IT services. Most commonly used in UK Government departments.
IT Infrastructure	All of the hardware, software, networks, facilities etc. that are required to Develop, Test, deliver, Monitor, Control or support IT Services. The term IT Infrastructure includes all of the Information Technology but not the associated people, Processes and documentation.

IT Operations	(Service Operation) Activities carried out by IT Operations Control, including Console Management, Job Scheduling, Backup and Restore, and Print and Output Management. IT Operations is also used as a synonym for Service Operation.
IT Operations Control	(Service Operation) The Function responsible for Monitoring and Control of the IT Services and IT Infrastructure. See Operations Bridge.
IT Operations Management	(Service Operation) The Function within an IT Service Provider which performs the daily Activities needed to manage IT Services and the supporting IT Infrastructure. IT Operations Management includes IT Operations Control and Facilities Management.
IT Service	A Service provided to one or more Customers by an IT Service Provider. An IT Service is based on the use of Information Technology and supports the Customer's Business Processes. An IT Service is made up from a combination of people, Processes and technology and should be defined in a Service Level Agreement.
IT Service Continuity Management (ITSCM)	(Service Design) The Process responsible for managing Risks that could seriously impact IT Services. ITSCM ensures that the IT Service Provider can always provide minimum agreed Service Levels, by reducing the Risk to an acceptable level and Planning for the Recovery of IT Services. ITSCM should be designed to support Business Continuity Management.
IT Service Continuity Plan	(Service Design) A Plan defining the steps required to Recover one or more IT Services. The Plan will also identify the triggers for Invocation, people to be involved, communications etc. The IT Service Continuity Plan should be part of a Business Continuity Plan.
IT Service Management (ITSM)	The implementation and management of Quality IT Services that meet the needs of the Business. IT Service Management is performed by IT Service Providers through an appropriate mix of people, Process and Information Technology. See Service Management.
IT Service Management Forum (itSMF)	The IT Service Management Forum is an independent Organization dedicated to promoting a professional approach to IT Service Management. The itSMF is a not-for-profit membership Organization with representation in many countries around the world (itSMF Chapters). The itSMF and its membership contribute to the development of ITIL and associated IT Service Management Standards. See http://www.itsmf.com/ for more information.
IT Service Provider	(Service Strategy) A Service Provider that provides IT Services to Internal Customers or External Customers.

IT Steering Group (ISG)   A formal group that is responsible for ensuring that Business and IT Service Provider Strategies and Plans are closely aligned. An IT Steering Group includes senior representatives from the Business and the IT Service Provider.

ITIL   A set of Best Practice guidance for IT Service Management. ITIL is owned by the OGC and consists of a series of publications giving guidance on the provision of Quality IT Services, and on the Processes and facilities needed to support them. See http://www.itil.co.uk/ for more information.

Job Description   A Document which defines the Roles, responsibilities, skills and knowledge required by a particular person. One Job Description can include multiple Roles, for example the Roles of Configuration Manager and Change Manager may be carried out by one person.

Job Scheduling   (Service Operation) Planning and managing the execution of software tasks that are required as part of an IT Service. Job Scheduling is carried out by IT Operations Management, and is often automated using software tools that run batch or online tasks at specific times of the day, week, month or year.

Kano Model   (Service Strategy) A Model developed by Noriaki Kano that is used to help understand Customer preferences. The Kano Model considers Attributes of an IT Service grouped into areas such as Basic Factors, Excitement Factors, Performance Factors etc.

Kepner & Tregoe Analysis   (Service Operation) (Continual Service Improvement) A structured approach to Problem solving. The Problem is analyzed in terms of what, where, when and extent. Possible causes are identified. The most probable cause is tested. The true cause is verified.

Key Performance Indicator (KPI)   (Continual Service Improvement) A Metric that is used to help manage a Process, IT Service or Activity. Many Metrics may be measured, but only the most important of these are defined as KPIs and used to actively manage and report on the Process, IT Service or Activity. KPIs should be selected to ensure that Efficiency, Effectiveness, and Cost Effectiveness are all managed. See Critical Success Factor.

Knowledge Base   (Service Transition) A logical database containing the data used by the Service Knowledge Management System.

Knowledge Management   (Service Transition) The Process responsible for gathering, analyzing, storing and sharing knowledge and information within an Organization. The primary purpose of Knowledge Management is to improve Efficiency by reducing the need to rediscover knowledge. See Data-to-Information-to-Knowledge-to-Wisdom, Service Knowledge Management System.

Known Error   (Service Operation) A Problem that has a documented Root Cause and a Workaround. Known Errors are created and managed throughout their Lifecycle by Problem Management. Known Errors may also be identified by Development or Suppliers.

Known Error Database (KEDB)	(Service Operation) A database containing all Known Error Records. This database is created by Problem Management and used by Incident and Problem Management. The Known Error Database is part of the Service Knowledge Management System.
Known Error Record	(Service Operation) A Record containing the details of a Known Error. Each Known Error Record documents the Lifecycle of a Known Error, including the Status, Root Cause and Workaround. In some implementations a Known Error is documented using additional fields in a Problem Record.
Lifecycle	The various stages in the life of an IT Service, Configuration Item, Incident, Problem, Change etc. The Lifecycle defines the Categories for Status and the Status transitions that are permitted. For example: • The Lifecycle of an Application includes Requirements, Design, Build, Deploy, Operate, Optimize. • The Expanded Incident Lifecycle includes Detect, Respond, Diagnose, Repair, Recover, Restore. • The lifecycle of a Server may include: Ordered, Received, In Test, Live, Disposed etc.
Line of Service (LOS)	(Service Strategy) A Core Service or Supporting Service that has multiple Service Level Packages. A line of Service is managed by a Product Manager and each Service Level Package is designed to support a particular market segment.
Live	(Service Transition) Refers to an IT Service or Configuration Item that is being used to deliver Service to a Customer.
Live Environment	(Service Transition) A controlled Environment containing Live Configuration Items used to deliver IT Services to Customers.
Maintainability	(Service Design) A measure of how quickly and Effectively a Configuration Item or IT Service can be restored to normal working after a Failure. Maintainability is often measured and reported as MTRS. Maintainability is also used in the context of Software or IT Service Development to mean ability to be Changed or Repaired easily.
Major Incident	(Service Operation) The highest Category of Impact for an Incident. A Major Incident results in significant disruption to the Business.
Managed Services	(Service Strategy) A perspective on IT Services which emphasizes the fact that they are managed. The term Managed Services is also used as a synonym for Outsourced IT Services.
Management Information	Information that is used to support decision making by managers. Management Information is often generated automatically by tools supporting the various IT Service Management Processes. Management Information often includes the values of KPIs such as "Percentage of Changes leading to Incidents", or "first time fix rate".

Management of Risk (MoR)	The OGC methodology for managing Risks. MoR includes all the Activities required to identify and Control the exposure to Risk which may have an impact on the achievement of an Organization's Business Objectives. See http://www.m-o-r.org/ for more details.
Management System	The framework of Policy, Processes and Functions that ensures an Organization can achieve its Objectives.
Manual Workaround	A Workaround that requires manual intervention. Manual Workaround is also used as the name of a Recovery Option in which The Business Process Operates without the use of IT Services. This is a temporary measure and is usually combined with another Recovery Option.
Marginal Cost	(Service Strategy) The Cost of continuing to provide the IT Service. Marginal Cost does not include investment already made, for example the cost of developing new software and delivering training.
Market Space	(Service Strategy) All opportunities that an IT Service Provider could exploit to meet business needs of Customers. The Market Space identifies the possible IT Services that an IT Service Provider may wish to consider delivering.
Maturity	(Continual Service Improvement) A measure of the Reliability, Efficiency and Effectiveness of a Process, Function, Organization etc. The most mature Processes and Functions are formally aligned to Business Objectives and Strategy, and are supported by a framework for continual improvement.
Maturity Level	A named level in a Maturity model such as the Carnegie Mellon Capability Maturity Model Integration.
Mean Time Between Failures (MTBF)	(Service Design) A Metric for measuring and reporting Reliability. MTBF is the average time that a Configuration Item or IT Service can perform its agreed Function without interruption. This is measured from when the CI or IT Service starts working, until it next fails.
Mean Time Between Service Incidents (MTBSI)	(Service Design) A Metric used for measuring and reporting Reliability. MTBSI is the mean time from when a System or IT Service fails, until it next fails. MTBSI is equal to MTBF + MTRS.
Mean Time To Repair (MTTR)	The average time taken to repair a Configuration Item or IT Service after a Failure. MTTR is measured from when the CI or IT Service fails until it is Repaired. MTTR does not include the time required to Recover or Restore. MTTR is sometimes incorrectly used to mean Mean Time to Restore Service.
Mean Time to Restore Service (MTRS)	The average time taken to Restore a Configuration Item or IT Service after a Failure. MTRS is measured from when the CI or IT Service fails until it is fully Restored and delivering its normal functionality. See Maintainability, Mean Time to Repair.

Metric   (Continual Service Improvement) Something that is measured and reported to help manage a Process, IT Service or Activity.
See KPI.

Middleware   (Service Design) Software that connects two or more software Components or Applications. Middleware is usually purchased from a Supplier, rather than developed within the IT Service Provider.
See Off the Shelf.

Mission Statement   The Mission Statement of an Organization is a short but complete description of the overall purpose and intentions of that Organization. It states what is to be achieved, but not how this should be done.

Model   A representation of a System, Process, IT Service, Configuration Item etc. that is used to help understand or predict future behavior.

Modeling   A technique that is used to predict the future behavior of a System, Process, IT Service, Configuration Item etc. Modeling is commonly used in Financial Management, Capacity Management and Availability Management.

Monitor Control Loop   (Service Operation) Monitoring the output of a Task, Process, IT Service or Configuration Item; comparing this output to a predefined norm; and taking appropriate action based on this comparison.

Monitoring   (Service Operation) Repeated observation of a Configuration Item, IT Service or Process to detect Events and to ensure that the current status is known.

Near-Shore   (Service Strategy) Provision of Services from a country near the country where the Customer is based. This can be the provision of an IT Service, or of supporting Functions such as Service Desk.
See On-shore, Off-shore.

Net Present Value (NPV)   (Service Strategy) A technique used to help make decisions about Capital Expenditure. NPV compares cash inflows to cash outflows. Positive NPV indicates that an investment is worthwhile.
See Internal Rate of Return, Return on Investment.

Notional Charging   (Service Strategy) An approach to Charging for IT Services. Charges to Customers are calculated and Customers are informed of the charge, but no money is actually transferred. Notional Charging is sometimes introduced to ensure that Customers are aware of the Costs they incur, or as a stage during the introduction of real Charging.

Objective   The defined purpose or aim of a Process, an Activity or an Organization as a whole. Objectives are usually expressed as measurable targets. The term Objective is also informally used to mean a Requirement.
See Outcome.

Off the Shelf	Synonym for Commercial Off the Shelf.
Office of Government Commerce (OGC)	OGC owns the ITIL brand (copyright and trademark). OGC is a UK Government department that supports the delivery of the government's procurement agenda through its work in collaborative procurement and in raising levels of procurement skills and capability with departments. It also provides support for complex public sector projects.
Office of Public Sector Information (OPSI)	OPSI license the Crown Copyright material used in the ITIL publications. They are a UK Government department who provide online access to UK legislation, license the re-use of Crown copyright material, manage the Information Fair Trader Scheme, maintain the Government's Information Asset Register and provide advice and guidance on official publishing and Crown copyright.
Off-shore	(Service Strategy) Provision of Services from a location outside the country where the Customer is based, often in a different continent. This can be the provision of an IT Service, or of supporting Functions such as Service Desk. See On-shore, Near-shore.
On-shore	(Service Strategy) Provision of Services from a location within the country where the Customer is based. See Off-shore, Near-shore.
Operate	To perform as expected. A Process or Configuration Item is said to Operate if it is delivering the Required outputs. Operate also means to perform one or more Operations. For example, to Operate a computer is to do the day-to-day Operations needed for it to perform as expected.
Operation	(Service Operation) Day-to-day management of an IT Service, System, or other Configuration Item. Operation is also used to mean any pre-defined Activity or Transaction. For example loading a magnetic tape, accepting money at a point of sale, or reading data from a disk drive.
Operational	The lowest of three levels of Planning and delivery (Strategic, Tactical, Operational). Operational Activities include the day-to-day or short term Planning or delivery of a Business Process or IT Service Management Process. The term Operational is also a synonym for Live.
Operational Cost	Cost resulting from running the IT Services. Often repeating payments. For example staff costs, hardware maintenance and electricity (also known as "current expenditure" or "revenue expenditure"). See Capital Expenditure.
Operational Expenditure (OPEX)	Synonym for Operational Cost.

Operational Level Agreement (OLA)	(Service Design) (Continual Service Improvement) An Agreement between an IT Service Provider and another part of the same Organization. An OLA supports the IT Service Provider's delivery of IT Services to Customers. The OLA defines the goods or Services to be provided and the responsibilities of both parties. For example there could be an OLA • between the IT Service Provider and a procurement department to obtain hardware in agreed times • between the Service Desk and a Support Group to provide Incident Resolution in agreed times. See Service Level Agreement.
Operations Bridge	(Service Operation) A physical location where IT Services and IT Infrastructure are monitored and managed.
Operations Control	Synonym for IT Operations Control.
Operations Management	Synonym for IT Operations Management.
Opportunity Cost	(Service Strategy) A Cost that is used in deciding between investment choices. Opportunity Cost represents the revenue that would have been generated by using the Resources in a different way. For example the Opportunity Cost of purchasing a new Server may include not carrying out a Service Improvement activity that the money could have been spent on. Opportunity cost analysis is used as part of a decision making processes, but is not treated as an actual Cost in any financial statement.
Optimize	Review, Plan and request Changes, in order to obtain the maximum Efficiency and Effectiveness from a Process, Configuration Item, Application etc.
Organization	A company, legal entity or other institution. Examples of Organizations that are not companies include International Standards Organization or itSMF. The term Organization is sometimes used to refer to any entity which has People, Resources and Budgets. For example a Project or Business Unit.
Outcome	The result of carrying out an Activity; following a Process; delivering an IT Service etc. The term Outcome is used to refer to intended results, as well as to actual results. See Objective.
Outsourcing	(Service Strategy) Using an External Service Provider to manage IT Services. See Service Sourcing, Type III Service Provider.
Overhead	Synonym for Indirect cost
Pain Value Analysis	(Service Operation) A technique used to help identify the Business Impact of one or more Problems. A formula is used to calculate Pain Value based on the number of Users affected, the duration of the Downtime, the Impact on each User, and the cost to the Business (if known).

Pareto Principle	(Service Operation) A technique used to priorities Activities. The Pareto Principle says that 80% of the value of any Activity is created with 20% of the effort. Pareto Analysis is also used in Problem Management to priorities possible Problem causes for investigation.
Partnership	A relationship between two Organizations which involves working closely together for common goals or mutual benefit. The IT Service Provider should have a Partnership with the Business, and with Third Parties who are critical to the delivery of IT Services. See Value Network.
Passive Monitoring	(Service Operation) Monitoring of a Configuration Item, an IT Service or a Process that relies on an Alert or notification to discover the current status. See Active Monitoring.
Pattern of Business Activity (PBA)	(Service Strategy) A Workload profile of one or more Business Activities. Patterns of Business Activity are used to help the IT Service Provider understand and plan for different levels of Business Activity. See User Profile.
Percentage utilization	(Service Design) The amount of time that a Component is busy over a given period of time. For example, if a CPU is busy for 1800 seconds in a one hour period, its utilization is 50%
Performance	A measure of what is achieved or delivered by a System, person, team, Process, or IT Service.
Performance Anatomy	(Service Strategy) An approach to Organizational Culture that integrates, and actively manages, leadership and strategy, people development, technology enablement, performance management and innovation.
Performance Management	(Continual Service Improvement) The Process responsible for day-to-day Capacity Management Activities. These include Monitoring, Threshold detection, Performance analysis and Tuning, and implementing Changes related to Performance and Capacity.
Pilot	(Service Transition) A limited Deployment of an IT Service, a Release or a Process to the Live Environment. A Pilot is used to reduce Risk and to gain User feedback and Acceptance. See Test, Evaluation.
Plan	A detailed proposal which describes the Activities and Resources needed to achieve an Objective. For example a Plan to implement a new IT Service or Process. ISO/IEC 20000 requires a Plan for the management of each IT Service Management Process.

Plan-Do-Check-Act	(Continual Service Improvement) A four stage cycle for Process management, attributed to Edward Deming. Plan-Do-Check-Act is also called the Deming Cycle. PLAN: Design or revise Processes that support the IT Services. DO: Implement the Plan and manage the Processes. CHECK: Measure the Processes and IT Services, compare with Objectives and produce reports ACT: Plan and implement Changes to improve the Processes.
Planned Downtime	(Service Design) Agreed time when an IT Service will not be available. Planned Downtime is often used for maintenance, upgrades and testing. See Change Window, Downtime.
Planning	An Activity responsible for creating one or more Plans. For example, Capacity Planning.
PMBOK	A Project management Standard maintained and published by the Project Management Institute. PMBOK stands for Project Management Body of Knowledge. See http://www.pmi.org/ for more information. See PRINCE2.
Policy	Formally documented management expectations and intentions. Policies are used to direct decisions, and to ensure consistent and appropriate development and implementation of Processes, Standards, Roles, Activities, IT Infrastructure etc.
Portable Facility	(Service Design) A prefabricated building, or a large vehicle, provided by a Third Party and moved to a site when needed by an IT Service Continuity Plan. See Recovery Option, Fixed Facility.
Post Implementation Review (PIR)	A Review that takes place after a Change or a Project has been implemented. A PIR determines if the Change or Project was successful, and identifies opportunities for improvement.
Practice	A way of working, or a way in which work must be done. Practices can include Activities, Processes, Functions, Standards and Guidelines. See Best Practice.
Prerequisite for Success (PFS)	An Activity that needs to be completed, or a condition that needs to be met, to enable successful implementation of a Plan or Process. A PFS is often an output from one Process that is a required input to another Process.
Pricing	(Service Strategy) The Activity for establishing how much Customers will be Charged.
PRINCE2	The standard UK government methodology for Project management. See http://www.ogc.gov.uk/prince2/ for more information. See PMBOK.

| Priority | (Service Transition) (Service Operation) A Category used to identify the relative importance of an Incident, Problem or Change. Priority is based on Impact and Urgency, and is used to identify required times for actions to be taken. For example the SLA may state that Priority2 Incidents must be resolved within 12 hours. |

Proactive Monitoring
(Service Operation) Monitoring that looks for patterns of Events to predict possible future Failures.
See Reactive Monitoring.

Proactive Problem Management
(Service Operation) Part of the Problem Management Process. The Objective of Proactive Problem Management is to identify Problems that might otherwise be missed. Proactive Problem Management analyses Incident Records, and uses data collected by other IT Service Management Processes to identify trends or significant Problems.

Problem
(Service Operation) A cause of one or more Incidents. The cause is not usually known at the time a Problem Record is created, and the Problem Management Process is responsible for further investigation.

Problem Management
(Service Operation) The Process responsible for managing the Lifecycle of all Problems. The primary Objectives of Problem Management are to prevent Incidents from happening, and to minimize the Impact of Incidents that cannot be prevented.

Problem Record
(Service Operation) A Record containing the details of a Problem. Each Problem Record documents the Lifecycle of a single Problem.

Procedure
A Document containing steps that specify how to achieve an Activity. Procedures are defined as part of Processes.
See Work Instruction.

Process
A structured set of Activities designed to accomplish a specific Objective. A Process takes one or more defined inputs and turns them into defined outputs. A Process may include any of the Roles, responsibilities, tools and management Controls required to reliably deliver the outputs. A Process may define Policies, Standards, Guidelines, Activities, and Work Instructions if they are needed.

Process Control
The Activity of planning and regulating a Process, with the Objective of performing the Process in an Effective, Efficient, and consistent manner.

Process Manager
A Role responsible for Operational management of a Process. The Process Manager's responsibilities include Planning and coordination of all Activities required to carry out, monitor and report on the Process. There may be several Process Managers for one Process, for example regional Change Managers or IT Service Continuity Managers for each data centre. The Process Manager Role is often assigned to the person who carries out the Process Owner Role, but the two Roles may be separate in larger Organizations.

Process Owner	A Role responsible for ensuring that a Process is Fit for Purpose. The Process Owner's responsibilities include sponsorship, Design, Change Management and continual improvement of the Process and its Metrics. This Role is often assigned to the same person who carries out the Process Manager Role, but the two Roles may be separate in larger Organizations.
Production Environment	Synonym for Live Environment.
Profit Centre	(Service Strategy) A Business Unit which charges for Services provided. A Profit Centre can be created with the objective of making a profit, recovering Costs, or running at a loss. An IT Service Provider can be run as a Cost Centre or a Profit Centre.
pro-forma	A template, or example Document containing example data that will be replaced with the real values when these are available.
Program	A number of Projects and Activities that are planned and managed together to achieve an overall set of related Objectives and other Outcomes.
Project	A temporary Organization, with people and other Assets required to achieve an Objective or other Outcome. Each Project has a Lifecycle that typically includes initiation, Planning, execution, Closure etc. Projects are usually managed using a formal methodology such as PRINCE2.
Projected Service Outage (PSO)	(Service Transition) A Document that identifies the effect of planned Changes, maintenance Activities and Test Plans on agreed Service Levels.
PRojects IN Controlled Environments (PRINCE2)	See PRINCE2
Qualification	(Service Transition) An Activity that ensures that IT Infrastructure is appropriate, and correctly configured, to support an Application or IT Service. See Validation.
Quality	The ability of a product, Service, or Process to provide the intended value. For example, a hardware Component can be considered to be of high Quality if it performs as expected and delivers the required Reliability. Process Quality also requires an ability to monitor Effectiveness and Efficiency, and to improve them if necessary. See Quality Management System.
Quality Assurance (QA)	(Service Transition) The Process responsible for ensuring that the Quality of a product, Service or Process will provide its intended Value.
Quality Management System (QMS)	(Continual Service Improvement) The set of Processes responsible for ensuring that all work carried out by an Organization is of a suitable Quality to reliably meet Business Objectives or Service Levels. See ISO 9000.

Quick Win	(Continual Service Improvement) An improvement Activity which is expected to provide a Return on Investment in a short period of time with relatively small Cost and effort. See Pareto Principle.
RACI	(Service Design) (Continual Service Improvement) A Model used to help define Roles and Responsibilities. RACI stands for Responsible, Accountable, Consulted and Informed. See Stakeholder.
Reactive Monitoring	(Service Operation) Monitoring that takes action in response to an Event. For example submitting a batch job when the previous job completes, or logging an Incident when an Error occurs. See Proactive Monitoring.
Reciprocal Arrangement	(Service Design) A Recovery Option. An agreement between two Organizations to share resources in an emergency. For example, Computer Room space or use of a mainframe.
Record	A Document containing the results or other output from a Process or Activity. Records are evidence of the fact that an Activity took place and may be paper or electronic. For example, an Audit report, an Incident Record, or the minutes of a meeting.
Recovery	(Service Design) (Service Operation) Returning a Configuration Item or an IT Service to a working state. Recovery of an IT Service often includes recovering data to a known consistent state. After Recovery, further steps may be needed before the IT Service can be made available to the Users (Restoration).
Recovery Option	(Service Design) A Strategy for responding to an interruption to Service. Commonly used Strategies are Do Nothing, Manual Workaround, Reciprocal Arrangement, Gradual Recovery, Intermediate Recovery, Fast Recovery, Immediate Recovery. Recovery Options may make use of dedicated facilities, or Third Party facilities shared by multiple Businesses.
Recovery Point Objective (RPO)	(Service Operation) The maximum amount of data that may be lost when Service is Restored after an interruption. Recovery Point Objective is expressed as a length of time before the Failure. For example a Recovery Point Objective of one day may be supported by daily Backups, and up to 24 hours of data may be lost. Recovery Point Objectives for each IT Service should be negotiated, agreed and documented, and used as Requirements for Service Design and IT Service Continuity Plans.
Recovery Time Objective (RTO)	(Service Operation) The maximum time allowed for recovery of an IT Service following an interruption. The Service Level to be provided may be less than normal Service Level Targets. Recovery Time Objectives for each IT Service should be negotiated, agreed and documented. See Business Impact Analysis.

Redundancy	Synonym for Fault Tolerance. The term Redundant also has a generic meaning of obsolete, or no longer needed.
Relationship	A connection or interaction between two people or things. In Business Relationship Management it is the interaction between the IT Service Provider and the Business. In Configuration Management it is a link between two Configuration Items that identifies a dependency or connection between them. For example Applications may be linked to the Servers they run on, IT Services have many links to all the CIs that contribute to them.
Relationship Processes	The ISO/IEC 20000 Process group that includes Business Relationship Management and Supplier Management.
Release	(Service Transition) A collection of hardware, software, documentation, Processes or other Components required to implement one or more approved Changes to IT Services. The contents of each Release are managed, Tested, and Deployed as a single entity.
Release and Deployment Management	(Service Transition) The Process responsible for both Release Management and Deployment.
Release Identification	(Service Transition) A naming convention used to uniquely identify a Release. The Release Identification typically includes a reference to the Configuration Item and a version number. For example Microsoft Office 2003 SR2.
Release Management	(Service Transition) The Process responsible for Planning, scheduling and controlling the movement of Releases to Test and Live Environments. The primary Objective of Release Management is to ensure that the integrity of the Live Environment is protected and that the correct Components are released. Release Management is part of the Release and Deployment Management Process.
Release Process	The name used by ISO/IEC 20000 for the Process group that includes Release Management. This group does not include any other Processes. Release Process is also used as a synonym for Release Management Process.
Release Record	(Service Transition) A Record in the CMDB that defines the content of a Release. A Release Record has Relationships with all Configuration Items that are affected by the Release.
Release Unit	(Service Transition) Components of an IT Service that are normally Released together. A Release Unit typically includes sufficient Components to perform a useful Function. For example one Release Unit could be a Desktop PC, including Hardware, Software, Licenses, Documentation etc. A different Release Unit may be the complete Payroll Application, including IT Operations Procedures and User training.

Release Window	Synonym for Change Window.
Reliability	(Service Design) (Continual Service Improvement) A measure of how long a Configuration Item or IT Service can perform its agreed Function without interruption. Usually measured as MTBF or MTBSI. The term Reliability can also be used to state how likely it is that a Process, Function etc. will deliver its required outputs. See Availability.
Remediation	(Service Transition) Recovery to a known state after a failed Change or Release.
Repair	(Service Operation) The replacement or correction of a failed Configuration Item.
Request for Change (RFC)	(Service Transition) A formal proposal for a Change to be made. An RFC includes details of the proposed Change, and may be recorded on paper or electronically. The term RFC is often misused to mean a Change Record, or the Change itself.
Request Fulfilment	(Service Operation) The Process responsible for managing the Lifecycle of all Service Requests.
Requirement	(Service Design) A formal statement of what is needed. For example a Service Level Requirement, a Project Requirement or the required Deliverables for a Process. See Statement of Requirements.
Resilience	(Service Design) The ability of a Configuration Item or IT Service to resist Failure or to Recover quickly following a Failure. For example, an armored cable will resist failure when put under stress. See Fault Tolerance.
Resolution	(Service Operation) Action taken to repair the Root Cause of an Incident or Problem, or to implement a Workaround. In ISO/IEC 20000, Resolution Processes is the Process group that includes Incident and Problem Management.
Resolution Processes	The ISO/IEC 20000 Process group that includes Incident Management and Problem Management.
Resource	(Service Strategy) A generic term that includes IT Infrastructure, people, money or anything else that might help to deliver an IT Service. Resources are considered to be Assets of an Organization. See Capability, Service Asset.
Response Time	A measure of the time taken to complete an Operation or Transaction. Used in Capacity Management as a measure of IT Infrastructure Performance, and in Incident Management as a measure of the time taken to answer the phone, or to start Diagnosis.

Responsiveness	A measurement of the time taken to respond to something. This could be Response Time of a Transaction, or the speed with which an IT Service Provider responds to an Incident or Request for Change etc.
Restoration of Service	See Restore.
Restore	(Service Operation) Taking action to return an IT Service to the Users after Repair and Recovery from an Incident. This is the primary Objective of Incident Management.
Retire	(Service Transition) Permanent removal of an IT Service, or other Configuration Item, from the Live Environment. Retired is a stage in the Lifecycle of many Configuration Items.
Return on Investment (ROI)	(Service Strategy) (Continual Service Improvement) A measurement of the expected benefit of an investment. In the simplest sense it is the net profit of an investment divided by the net worth of the assets invested. See Net Present Value, Value on Investment.
Return to Normal	(Service Design) The phase of an IT Service Continuity Plan during which full normal operations are resumed. For example, if an alternate data centre has been in use, then this phase will bring the primary data centre back into operation, and restore the ability to invoke IT Service Continuity Plans again.
Review	An evaluation of a Change, Problem, Process, Project etc. Reviews are typically carried out at predefined points in the Lifecycle, and especially after Closure. The purpose of a Review is to ensure that all Deliverables have been provided, and to identify opportunities for improvement. See Post Implementation Review.
Rights	(Service Operation) Entitlements, or permissions, granted to a User or Role. For example the Right to modify particular data, or to authorize a Change.
Risk	A possible Event that could cause harm or loss, or affect the ability to achieve Objectives. A Risk is measured by the probability of a Threat, the Vulnerability of the Asset to that Threat, and the Impact it would have if it occurred.
Risk Assessment	The initial steps of Risk Management. Analyzing the value of Assets to the business, identifying Threats to those Assets, and evaluating how Vulnerable each Asset is to those Threats. Risk Assessment can be quantitative (based on numerical data) or qualitative.
Risk Management	The Process responsible for identifying, assessing and controlling Risks. See Risk Assessment.
Role	A set of responsibilities, Activities and authorities granted to a person or team. A Role is defined in a Process. One person or team may have multiple Roles, for example the Roles of Configuration Manager and Change Manager may be carried out by a single person.

Rollout	(Service Transition) Synonym for Deployment. Most often used to refer to complex or phased Deployments or Deployments to multiple locations.
Root Cause	(Service Operation) The underlying or original cause of an Incident or Problem.
Root Cause Analysis (RCA)	(Service Operation) An Activity that identifies the Root Cause of an Incident or Problem. RCA typically concentrates on IT Infrastructure failures. See Service Failure Analysis.
Running Costs	Synonym for Operational Costs
Scalability	The ability of an IT Service, Process, Configuration Item etc. to perform its agreed Function when the Workload or Scope changes.
Scope	The boundary, or extent, to which a Process, Procedure, Certification, Contract etc. applies. For example the Scope of Change Management may include all Live IT Services and related Configuration Items, the Scope of an ISO/IEC 20000 Certificate may include all IT Services delivered out of a named data centre.
Second-line Support	(Service Operation) The second level in a hierarchy of Support Groups involved in the resolution of Incidents and investigation of Problems. Each level contains more specialist skills, or has more time or other Resources.
Security	See Information Security Management
Security Management	Synonym for Information Security Management
Security Policy	Synonym for Information Security Policy
Separation of Concerns (SoC)	(Service Strategy) An approach to Designing a solution or IT Service that divides the problem into pieces that can be solved independently. This approach separates "what" is to be done from "how" it is to be done.
Server	(Service Operation) A computer that is connected to a network and provides software Functions that are used by other computers.
Service	A means of delivering value to Customers by facilitating Outcomes Customers want to achieve without the ownership of specific Costs and Risks.
Service Acceptance Criteria (SAC)	(Service Transition) A set of criteria used to ensure that an IT Service meets its functionality and Quality Requirements and that the IT Service Provider is ready to Operate the new IT Service when it has been Deployed. See Acceptance.
Service Analytics	(Service Strategy) A technique used in the Assessment of the Business Impact of Incidents. Service Analytics Models the dependencies between Configuration Items, and the dependencies of IT Services on Configuration Items.

Service Asset	Any Capability or Resource of a Service Provider. See Asset.
Service Asset and Configuration Management (SACM)	(Service Transition) The Process responsible for both Configuration Management and Asset Management.
Service Capacity Management (SCM)	(Service Design) (Continual Service Improvement) The Activity responsible for understanding the Performance and Capacity of IT Services. The Resources used by each IT Service and the pattern of usage over time are collected, recorded, and analyzed for use in the Capacity Plan. See Business Capacity Management, Component Capacity Management.
Service Catalogue	(Service Design) A database or structured Document with information about all Live IT Services, including those available for Deployment. The Service Catalogue is the only part of the Service Portfolio published to Customers, and is used to support the sale and delivery of IT Services. The Service Catalogue includes information about deliverables, prices, contact points, ordering and request Processes. See Contract Portfolio.
Service Continuity Management	Synonym for IT Service Continuity Management.
Service Contract	(Service Strategy) A Contract to deliver one or more IT Services. The term Service Contract is also used to mean any Agreement to deliver IT Services, whether this is a legal Contract or an SLA. See Contract Portfolio.
Service Culture	A Customer oriented Culture. The major Objectives of a Service Culture are Customer satisfaction and helping the Customer to achieve their Business Objectives.
Service Design	(Service Design) A stage in the Lifecycle of an IT Service. Service Design includes a number of Processes and Functions and is the title of one of the Core ITIL publications. See Design.
Service Design Package	(Service Design) Document(s) defining all aspects of an IT Service and its Requirements through each stage of its Lifecycle. A Service Design Package is produced for each new IT Service, major Change, or IT Service Retirement.
Service Desk	(Service Operation) The Single Point of Contact between the Service Provider and the Users. A typical Service Desk manages Incidents and Service Requests, and also handles communication with the Users.

Service Failure Analysis (SFA)	(Service Design) An Activity that identifies underlying causes of one or more IT Service interruptions. SFA identifies opportunities to improve the IT Service Provider's Processes and tools, and not just the IT Infrastructure. SFA is a time constrained, project-like activity, rather than an ongoing process of analysis. See Root Cause Analysis.
Service Hours	(Service Design) (Continual Service Improvement) An agreed time period when a particular IT Service should be Available. For example, "Monday-Friday 08:00 to 17:00 except public holidays". Service Hours should be defined in a Service Level Agreement.
Service Improvement Plan (SIP)	(Continual Service Improvement) A formal Plan to implement improvements to a Process or IT Service.
Service Knowledge Management System (SKMS)	(Service Transition) A set of tools and databases that are used to manage knowledge and information. The SKMS includes the Configuration Management System, as well as other tools and databases. The SKMS stores, manages, updates, and presents all information that an IT Service Provider needs to manage the full Lifecycle of IT Services.
Service Level	Measured and reported achievement against one or more Service Level Targets. The term Service Level is sometimes used informally to mean Service Level Target.
Service Level Agreement (SLA)	(Service Design) (Continual Service Improvement) An Agreement between an IT Service Provider and a Customer. The SLA describes the IT Service, documents Service Level Targets, and specifies the responsibilities of the IT Service Provider and the Customer. A single SLA may cover multiple IT Services or multiple Customers. See Operational Level Agreement.
Service Level Management (SLM)	(Service Design) (Continual Service Improvement) The Process responsible for negotiating Service Level Agreements, and ensuring that these are met. SLM is responsible for ensuring that all IT Service Management Processes, Operational Level Agreements, and Underpinning Contracts, are appropriate for the agreed Service Level Targets. SLM monitors and reports on Service Levels, and holds regular Customer reviews.
Service Level Package (SLP)	(Service Strategy) A defined level of Utility and Warranty for a particular Service Package. Each SLP is designed to meet the needs of a particular Pattern of Business Activity. See Line of Service.
Service Level Requirement (SLR)	(Service Design) (Continual Service Improvement) A Customer Requirement for an aspect of an IT Service. SLRs are based on Business Objectives and are used to negotiate agreed Service Level Targets.

Service Level Target	(Service Design) (Continual Service Improvement) A commitment that is documented in a Service Level Agreement. Service Level Targets are based on Service Level Requirements, and are needed to ensure that the IT Service design is Fit for Purpose. Service Level Targets should be SMART, and are usually based on KPIs.
Service Maintenance Objective	(Service Operation) The expected time that a Configuration Item will be unavailable due to planned maintenance Activity.
Service Management	Service Management is a set of specialized organizational capabilities for providing value to customers in the form of services.
Service Management Lifecycle	An approach to IT Service Management that emphasizes the importance of coordination and Control across the various Functions, Processes, and Systems necessary to manage the full Lifecycle of IT Services. The Service Management Lifecycle approach considers the Strategy, Design, Transition, Operation and Continuous Improvement of IT Services.
Service Manager	A manager who is responsible for managing the end-to-end Lifecycle of one or more IT Services. The term Service Manager is also used to mean any manager within the IT Service Provider. Most commonly used to refer to a Business Relationship Manager, a Process Manager, an Account Manager or a senior manager with responsibility for IT Services overall.
Service Operation	(Service Operation) A stage in the Lifecycle of an IT Service. Service Operation includes a number of Processes and Functions and is the title of one of the Core ITIL publications. See Operation.
Service Owner	(Continual Service Improvement) A Role which is accountable for the delivery of a specific IT Service.
Service Package	(Service Strategy) A detailed description of an IT Service that is available to be delivered to Customers. A Service Package includes a Service Level Package and one or more Core Services and Supporting Services.
Service Pipeline	(Service Strategy) A database or structured Document listing all IT Services that are under consideration or Development, but are not yet available to Customers. The Service Pipeline provides a Business view of possible future IT Services and is part of the Service Portfolio which is not normally published to Customers.
Service Portfolio	(Service Strategy) The complete set of Services that are managed by a Service Provider. The Service Portfolio is used to manage the entire Lifecycle of all Services, and includes three Categories: Service Pipeline (proposed or in Development); Service Catalogue (Live or available for Deployment); and Retired Services. See Service Portfolio Management, Contract Portfolio.
Service Portfolio Management (SPM)	(Service Strategy) The Process responsible for managing the Service Portfolio. Service Portfolio Management considers Services in terms of the Business value that they provide.

Service Potential	(Service Strategy) The total possible value of the overall Capabilities and Resources of the IT Service Provider.
Service Provider	(Service Strategy) An Organization supplying Services to one or more Internal Customers or External Customers. Service Provider is often used as an abbreviation for IT Service Provider. See Type I Service Provider, Type II Service Provider, Type III Service Provider.
Service Provider Interface (SPI)	(Service Strategy) An interface between the IT Service Provider and a User, Customer, Business Process, or a Supplier. Analysis of Service Provider Interfaces helps to coordinate end-to-end management of IT Services.
Service Provisioning Optimization (SPO)	(Service Strategy) Analyzing the finances and constraints of an IT Service to decide if alternative approaches to Service delivery might reduce Costs or improve Quality.
Service Reporting	(Continual Service Improvement) The Process responsible for producing and delivering reports of achievement and trends against Service Levels. Service Reporting should agree the format, content and frequency of reports with Customers.
Service Request	(Service Operation) A request from a User for information, or advice, or for a Standard Change or for Access to an IT Service. For example to reset a password, or to provide standard IT Services for a new User. Service Requests are usually handled by a Service Desk, and do not require an RFC to be submitted. See Request Fulfilment.
Service Sourcing	(Service Strategy) The Strategy and approach for deciding whether to provide a Service internally or to Outsource it to an External Service Provider. Service Sourcing also means the execution of this Strategy. Service Sourcing includes: <ul><li>Internal Sourcing - Internal or Shared Services using Type I or Type II Service Providers.</li><li>Traditional Sourcing - Full Service Outsourcing using a Type III Service Provider.</li><li>Multivendor Sourcing - Prime, Consortium or Selective Outsourcing using Type III Service Providers.</li></ul>
Service Strategy	(Service Strategy) The title of one of the Core ITIL publications. Service Strategy establishes an overall Strategy for IT Services and for IT Service Management.
Service Transition	(Service Transition) A stage in the Lifecycle of an IT Service. Service Transition includes a number of Processes and Functions and is the title of one of the Core ITIL publications. See Transition.

Service Utility	(Service Strategy) The Functionality of an IT Service from the Customer's perspective. The Business value of an IT Service is created by the combination of Service Utility (what the Service does) and Service Warranty (how well it does it). See Utility.
Service Validation and Testing	(Service Transition) The Process responsible for Validation and Testing of a new or Changed IT Service. Service Validation and Testing ensures that the IT Service matches its Design Specification and will meet the needs of the Business.
Service Valuation	(Service Strategy) A measurement of the total Cost of delivering an IT Service, and the total value to the Business of that IT Service. Service Valuation is used to help the Business and the IT Service Provider agree on the value of the IT Service.
Service Warranty	(Service Strategy) Assurance that an IT Service will meet agreed Requirements. This may be a formal Agreement such as a Service Level Agreement or Contract, or may be a marketing message or brand image. The Business value of an IT Service is created by the combination of Service Utility (what the Service does) and Service Warranty (how well it does it). See Warranty.
Serviceability	(Service Design) (Continual Service Improvement) The ability of a Third Party Supplier to meet the terms of their Contract. This Contract will include agreed levels of Reliability, Maintainability or Availability for a Configuration Item.
Shift	(Service Operation) A group or team of people who carry out a specific Role for a fixed period of time. For example there could be four shifts of IT Operations Control personnel to support an IT Service that is used 24 hours a day.
Simulation modeling	(Service Design) (Continual Service Improvement) A technique that creates a detailed Model to predict the behavior of a Configuration Item or IT Service. Simulation Models can be very accurate but are expensive and time consuming to create. A Simulation Model is often created by using the actual Configuration Items that are being modeled, with artificial Workloads or Transactions. They are used in Capacity Management when accurate results are important. A simulation model is sometimes called a Performance Benchmark.
Single Point of Contact	(Service Operation) Providing a single consistent way to communicate with an Organization or Business Unit. For example, a Single Point of Contact for an IT Service Provider is usually called a Service Desk.

Single Point of Failure (SPOF)	(Service Design) Any Configuration Item that can cause an Incident when it fails, and for which a Countermeasure has not been implemented. A SPOF may be a person, or a step in a Process or Activity, as well as a Component of the IT Infrastructure. See Failure.
SLAM Chart	(Continual Service Improvement) A Service Level Agreement Monitoring Chart is used to help monitor and report achievements against Service Level Targets. A SLAM Chart is typically color coded to show whether each agreed Service Level Target has been met, missed, or nearly missed during each of the previous 12 months.
SMART	(Service Design) (Continual Service Improvement) An acronym for helping to remember that targets in Service Level Agreements and Project Plans should be Specific, Measurable, Achievable, Relevant and Timely.
Snapshot	(Service Transition) The current state of a Configuration as captured by a discovery tool. Also used as a synonym for Benchmark. See Baseline.
Source	See Service Sourcing.
Specification	A formal definition of Requirements. A Specification may be used to define technical or Operational Requirements, and may be internal or external. Many public Standards consist of a Code of Practice and a Specification. The Specification defines the Standard against which an Organization can be Audited.
Stakeholder	All people who have an interest in an Organization, Project, IT Service etc. Stakeholders may be interested in the Activities, targets, Resources, or Deliverables. Stakeholders may include Customers, Partners, employees, shareholders, owners, etc. See RACI.
Standard	A mandatory Requirement. Examples include ISO/IEC 20000 (an international Standard), an internal security Standard for Unix configuration, or a government Standard for how financial Records should be maintained. The term Standard is also used to refer to a Code of Practice or Specification published by a Standards Organization such as ISO or BSI. See Guideline.
Standard Change	(Service Transition) A pre-approved Change that is low Risk, relatively common and follows a Procedure or Work Instruction. For example password reset or provision of standard equipment to a new employee. RFCs are not required to implement a Standard Change, and they are logged and tracked using a different mechanism, such as a Service Request. See Change Model.

Standard Operating Procedures (SOP)	(Service Operation) Procedures used by IT Operations Management.
Standby	(Service Design) Used to refer to Resources that are not required to deliver the Live IT Services, but are available to support IT Service Continuity Plans. For example a Standby data centre may be maintained to support Hot Standby, Warm Standby or Cold Standby arrangements.
Statement of requirements (SOR)	(Service Design) A Document containing all Requirements for a product purchase, or a new or changed IT Service. See Terms of Reference.
Status	The name of a required field in many types of Record. It shows the current stage in the Lifecycle of the associated Configuration Item, Incident, Problem etc.
Status Accounting	(Service Transition) The Activity responsible for recording and reporting the Lifecycle of each Configuration Item.
Storage Management	(Service Operation) The Process responsible for managing the storage and maintenance of data throughout its Lifecycle.
Strategic	(Service Strategy) The highest of three levels of Planning and delivery (Strategic, Tactical, Operational). Strategic Activities include Objective setting and long term Planning to achieve the overall Vision.
Strategy	(Service Strategy) A Strategic Plan designed to achieve defined Objectives.
Super User	(Service Operation) A User who helps other Users, and assists in communication with the Service Desk or other parts of the IT Service Provider. Super Users typically provide support for minor Incidents and training.
Supplier	(Service Strategy) (Service Design) A Third Party responsible for supplying goods or Services that are required to deliver IT services. Examples of suppliers include commodity hardware and software vendors, network and telecom providers, and Outsourcing Organizations. See Underpinning Contract, Supply Chain.
Supplier and Contract Database (SCD)	(Service Design) A database or structured Document used to manage Supplier Contracts throughout their Lifecycle. The SCD contains key Attributes of all Contracts with Suppliers, and should be part of the Service Knowledge Management System.
Supplier Management	(Service Design) The Process responsible for ensuring that all Contracts with Suppliers support the needs of the Business, and that all Suppliers meet their contractual commitments.

Supply Chain

(Service Strategy) The Activities in a Value Chain carried out by Suppliers. A Supply Chain typically involves multiple Suppliers, each adding value to the product or Service.
See Value Network.

Support Group

(Service Operation) A group of people with technical skills. Support Groups provide the Technical Support needed by all of the IT Service Management Processes.
See Technical Management.

Support Hours

(Service Design) (Service Operation) The times or hours when support is available to the Users. Typically this is the hours when the Service Desk is available. Support Hours should be defined in a Service Level Agreement, and may be different from Service Hours. For example, Service Hours may be 24 hours a day, but the Support Hours may be 07:00 to 19:00.

Supporting Service

(Service Strategy) A Service that enables or enhances a Core Service. For example a Directory Service or a Backup Service.
See Service Package.

SWOT Analysis

(Continual Service Improvement) A technique that reviews and analyses the internal strengths and weaknesses of an Organization and the external opportunities and threats which it faces SWOT stands for Strengths, Weaknesses, Opportunities and Threats.

System

A number of related things that work together to achieve an overall Objective. For example:
- A computer System including hardware, software and Applications.
- A management System, including multiple Processes that are planned and managed together. For example a Quality Management System.
- A Database Management System or Operating System that includes many software modules that are designed to perform a set of related Functions.

System Management

The part of IT Service Management that focuses on the management of IT Infrastructure rather than Process.

Tactical

The middle of three levels of Planning and delivery (Strategic, Tactical, Operational). Tactical Activities include the medium term Plans required to achieve specific Objectives, typically over a period of weeks to months.

Tag

(Service Strategy) A short code used to identify a Category. For example tags EC1, EC2, EC3 etc. might be used to identify different Customer outcomes when analyzing and comparing Strategies. The term Tag is also used to refer to the Activity of assigning Tags to things.

Technical Management

(Service Operation) The Function responsible for providing technical skills in support of IT Services and management of the IT Infrastructure. Technical Management defines the Roles of Support Groups, as well as the tools, Processes and Procedures required.

Technical Observation (TO)	(Continual Service Improvement) A technique used in Service Improvement, Problem investigation and Availability Management. Technical support staff meet to monitor the behavior and Performance of an IT Service and make recommendations for improvement.
Technical Service	Synonym for Infrastructure Service.
Technical Support	Synonym for Technical Management.
Tension Metrics	(Continual Service Improvement) A set of related Metrics, in which improvements to one Metric have a negative effect on another. Tension Metrics are designed to ensure that an appropriate balance is achieved.
Terms of Reference (TOR)	(Service Design) A Document specifying the Requirements, Scope, Deliverables, Resources and schedule for a Project or Activity.
Test	(Service Transition) An Activity that verifies that a Configuration Item, IT Service, Process, etc. meets its Specification or agreed Requirements. See Service Validation and Testing, Acceptance.
Test Environment	(Service Transition) A controlled Environment used to Test Configuration Items, Builds, IT Services, Processes etc.
Third Party	A person, group, or Business who is not part of the Service Level Agreement for an IT Service, but is required to ensure successful delivery of that IT Service. For example a software Supplier, a hardware maintenance company, or a facilities department. Requirements for Third Parties are typically specified in Underpinning Contracts or Operational Level Agreements.
Third-line Support	(Service Operation) The third level in a hierarchy of Support Groups involved in the resolution of Incidents and investigation of Problems. Each level contains more specialist skills, or has more time or other Resources.
Threat	Anything that might exploit a Vulnerability. Any potential cause of an Incident can be considered to be a Threat. For example a fire is a Threat that could exploit the Vulnerability of flammable floor coverings. This term is commonly used in Information Security Management and IT Service Continuity Management, but also applies to other areas such as Problem and Availability Management.
Threshold	The value of a Metric which should cause an Alert to be generated, or management action to be taken. For example "Priority1 Incident not solved within 4 hours", "more than 5 soft disk errors in an hour", or "more than 10 failed changes in a month".
Throughput	(Service Design) A measure of the number of Transactions, or other Operations, performed in a fixed time. For example 5000 emails sent per hour, or 200 disk I/Os per second.

Total Cost of Ownership (TCO)	(Service Strategy) A methodology used to help make investment decisions. TCO assesses the full Lifecycle Cost of owning a Configuration Item, not just the initial Cost or purchase price. See Total Cost of Utilization.
Total Cost of Utilization (TCU)	(Service Strategy) A methodology used to help make investment and Service Sourcing decisions. TCU assesses the full Lifecycle Cost to the Customer of using an IT Service. See Total Cost of Ownership.
Total Quality Management (TQM)	(Continual Service Improvement) A methodology for managing continual Improvement by using a Quality Management System. TQM establishes a Culture involving all people in the Organization in a Process of continual monitoring and improvement.
Transaction	A discrete Function performed by an IT Service. For example transferring money from one bank account to another. A single Transaction may involve numerous additions, deletions and modifications of data. Either all of these complete successfully or none of them is carried out.
Transition	(Service Transition) A change in state, corresponding to a movement of an IT Service or other Configuration Item from one Lifecycle status to the next.
Transition Planning and Support	(Service Transition) The Process responsible for Planning all Service Transition Processes and co-coordinating the resources that they require. These Service Transition Processes are Change Management, Service Asset and Configuration Management, Release and Deployment Management, Service Validation and Testing, Evaluation, and Knowledge Management.
Trend Analysis	(Continual Service Improvement) Analysis of data to identify time related patterns. Trend Analysis is used in Problem Management to identify common Failures or fragile Configuration Items, and in Capacity Management as a Modeling tool to predict future behavior. It is also used as a management tool for identifying deficiencies in IT Service Management Processes.
Tuning	The Activity responsible for Planning Changes to make the most efficient use of Resources. Tuning is part of Performance Management, which also includes Performance Monitoring and implementation of the required Changes.
Type I Service Provider	(Service Strategy) An Internal Service Provider that is embedded within a Business Unit. There may be several Type I Service Providers within an Organization.
Type II Service Provider	(Service Strategy) An Internal Service Provider that provides shared IT Services to more than one Business Unit.

Type III Service Provider	(Service Strategy) A Service Provider that provides IT Services to External Customers.
Underpinning Contract (UC)	(Service Design) A Contract between an IT Service Provider and a Third Party. The Third Party provides goods or Services that support delivery of an IT Service to a Customer. The Underpinning Contract defines targets and responsibilities that are required to meet agreed Service Level Targets in an SLA.
Unit Cost	(Service Strategy) The Cost to the IT Service Provider of providing a single Component of an IT Service. For example the Cost of a single desktop PC, or of a single Transaction.
Urgency	(Service Transition) (Service Design) A measure of how long it will be until an Incident, Problem or Change has a significant Impact on the Business. For example a high Impact Incident may have low Urgency, if the Impact will not affect the Business until the end of the financial year. Impact and Urgency are used to assign Priority.
Usability	(Service Design) The ease with which an Application, product, or IT Service can be used. Usability Requirements are often included in a Statement of Requirements.
Use Case	(Service Design) A technique used to define required functionality and Objectives, and to Design Tests. Use Cases define realistic scenarios that describe interactions between Users and an IT Service or other System. See Change Case.
User	A person who uses the IT Service on a day-to-day basis. Users are distinct from Customers, as some Customers do not use the IT Service directly.
User Profile (UP)	(Service Strategy) A pattern of User demand for IT Services. Each User Profile includes one or more Patterns of Business Activity.
Utility	(Service Strategy) Functionality offered by a Product or Service to meet a particular need. Utility is often summarized as "what it does". See Service Utility.
Validation	(Service Transition) An Activity that ensures a new or changed IT Service, Process, Plan, or other Deliverable meets the needs of the Business. Validation ensures that Business Requirements are met even though these may have changed since the original Design. See Verification, Acceptance, Qualification, Service Validation and Testing.
Value Chain	(Service Strategy) A sequence of Processes that creates a product or Service that is of value to a Customer. Each step of the sequence builds on the previous steps and contributes to the overall product or Service. See Value Network.

Value for Money

An informal measure of Cost Effectiveness. Value for Money is often based on a comparison with the Cost of alternatives.
See Cost Benefit Analysis.

Value Network

(Service Strategy) A complex set of Relationships between two or more groups or organizations. Value is generated through exchange of knowledge, information, goods or Services.
See Value Chain, Partnership.

Value on Investment (VOI)

(Continual Service Improvement) A measurement of the expected benefit of an investment. VOI considers both financial and intangible benefits.
See Return on Investment.

Variable Cost

(Service Strategy) A Cost that depends on how much the IT Service is used, how many products are produced, the number and type of Users, or something else that cannot be fixed in advance.
See Variable Cost Dynamics.

Variable Cost Dynamics

(Service Strategy) A technique used to understand how overall Costs are impacted by the many complex variable elements that contribute to the provision of IT Services.

Variance

The difference between a planned value and the actual measured value. Commonly used in Financial Management, Capacity Management and Service Level Management, but could apply in any area where Plans are in place.

Verification

(Service Transition) An Activity that ensures a new or changed IT Service, Process, Plan, or other Deliverable is complete, accurate, Reliable and matches its Design Specification.
See Validation, Acceptance, Service Validation and Testing.

Verification and Audit

(Service Transition) The Activities responsible for ensuring that information in the CMDB is accurate and that all Configuration Items have been identified and recorded in the CMDB. Verification includes routine checks that are part of other Processes. For example, verifying the serial number of a desktop PC when a User logs an Incident. Audit is a periodic, formal check.

Version

(Service Transition) A Version is used to identify a specific Baseline of a Configuration Item. Versions typically use a naming convention that enables the sequence or date of each Baseline to be identified. For example Payroll Application Version 3 contains updated functionality from Version 2.

Vision

A description of what the Organization intends to become in the future. A Vision is created by senior management and is used to help influence Culture and Strategic Planning.

Vital Business Function (VBF)	(Service Design) A Function of a Business Process which is critical to the success of the Business. Vital Business Functions are an important consideration of Business Continuity Management, IT Service Continuity Management and Availability Management.
Vulnerability	A weakness that could be exploited by a Threat. For example an open firewall port, a password that is never changed, or a flammable carpet. A missing Control is also considered to be a Vulnerability.
Warm Standby	Synonym for Intermediate Recovery.
Warranty	(Service Strategy) A promise or guarantee that a product or Service will meet its agreed Requirements. See Service Validation and Testing, Service Warranty.
Work in Progress (WIP)	A Status that means Activities have started but are not yet complete. It is commonly used as a Status for Incidents, Problems, Changes etc.
Work Instruction	A Document containing detailed instructions that specify exactly what steps to follow to carry out an Activity. A Work Instruction contains much more detail than a Procedure and is only created if very detailed instructions are needed.
Workaround	(Service Operation) Reducing or eliminating the Impact of an Incident or Problem for which a full Resolution is not yet available. For example by restarting a failed Configuration Item. Workarounds for Problems are documented in Known Error Records. Workarounds for Incidents that do not have associated Problem Records are documented in the Incident Record.
Workload	The Resources required to deliver an identifiable part of an IT Service. Workloads may be Categorized by Users, groups of Users, or Functions within the IT Service. This is used to assist in analyzing and managing the Capacity, Performance and Utilization of Configuration Items and IT Services. The term Workload is sometimes used as a synonym for Throughput.

References

Bon, J. van (ed.) (2007). *Foundations of IT Service Management - based on ITIL V3*. Zaltbommel: Van Haren Publishing

Office of Government Commerce (2007). *ITIL: Service Transition*. London: The Stationary Office

Office of Government Commerce (2007). *Glossary ITIL Version 3*: http://www.best-management-practice.com

Index

ISO/IEC 20000
The Official Books from itSMF

ISO/IEC 20000: An Introduction
Promoting awareness of the certification for organizations within the IT Service Management environment.
ISBN: 978 908753081 5 (ENGLISH EDITION)
PRICE €49.95 EXCL TAX

Implementing ISO/IEC 20000 Certification:
The Roadmap
Practical advice, to assist readers through the requirements of the standard, the scoping, the project approach, the certification procedure and management of the certification.
ISBN: 978 908753082 2
PRICE €39.95 EXCL TAX

ISO/IEC 20000: A Pocket Guide
A quick and accessible guide to the fundamental requirements for corporate certification.
ISBN: 978 907721279 0 (ENGLISH EDITION)
PRICE €14.95 EXCL TAX

Other leading ITSM Books from itSMF

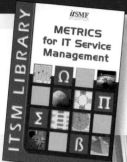

Metrics for IT Service Management

A general guide to the use of metrics as a mechanism to control and steer IT service organizations, with consideration of the design and implementation of metrics in service organizations using industry standard frameworks.

ISBN: 978 907721269 1

PRICE €39.95 EXCL TAX

Six Sigma for IT Management

The first book to provide a coherent view and guidance for using the Six Sigma approach successfully in IT Service Management, whilst aiming to merge both Six Sigma and ITIL® into a single unified approach to continuous improvement. Six Sigma for IT Management: A Pocket Guide is also available.

ISBN: 978 907721230 1 (ENGLISH EDITION)

PRICE €39.95 EXCL TAX

Frameworks for IT Management

An unparalleled guide to the myriad of IT management instruments currently available to IT and business managers. Frameworks for IT Management: A Pocket Guide is also available.

ISBN: 978 907721290 5 (ENGLISH EDITION)

PRICE €39.95 EXCL TAX

IT Governance based on CobiT 4.1: A Management Guide

Detailed information on the overall process model as well as the theory behind it.

ISBN: 978 90 8753116 4 (ENGLISH EDITION)

PRICE €20,75 EXCL TAX